Interpreting inte

FRANK J. HARRINGTON
GRAHAM H. TURNER

Interpreting interpreting
Studies and reflections on sign language interpreting

Forewords by Marina McIntire and Franz Pöchhacker

with

Ros Bramwell
Richard K. Brown
Jennifer Harris
Maureen Reed
Granville Tate
Caroline Taylor

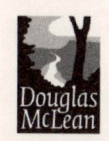

Douglas McLean

Coleford · England

© The authors 2001

First published in 2001
All rights reserved.
No part of this publication may be reproduced, stored in a retrieval system, transmitted or utilised in any form or by any means, electronic, mechanical, photocopying, recording or otherwise, without permission in writing from the Publishers:

Douglas McLean

8 St John Street
Coleford
Gloucestershire GL16 8RF
England
deafbooks@forestbooks.com
www.ForestBooks.com

British Library Cataloguing in Publication Data
A catalogue record for this book is available from the British Library
ISBN 0-946252-48-3

Typeset in 10/14pt Monotype Albertina
Typeset and printed by MFP Design and Print, Manchester
Typography and cover by Ernst Thoutenhoofd

Cover typeset in William C. in memory of William C. Stokoe

Contents

Preface: the campaign for real interpreting	vi
Foreword by Marina McIntire	xv
Foreword by Franz Pöchhacker	xvii

1 Reflections on constructing an interpreting profession

1	Rights and responsibilities: the relationship between Deaf people and interpreters	22
2	Regulation and responsibility: the relationship between interpreters and Deaf people	34
3	Agencies, interpreters and the Deaf community: working in harmony?	43
4	The code and the culture: sign language interpreting—in search of the new breed's ethics	53
5	Interpreting assignments: should I or shouldn't I?	67

2 Analyses of interpreting practices: Education

6	Deaf students and the interpreted classroom: the effect of translation on education?	74
7	The rise, fall and re-invention of the communicator: re-defining roles and responsibilities in educational interpreting	89

3 Analyses of interpreting practices: Health & social care

8	Deaf women: informed choice, policy and legislation	103
9	Interpreting in Social Services: setting the boundaries of good practice?	111

4 Analyses of interpreting practices: Law

10	The bilingual, bimodal courtroom: a first glance	124
11	Interaction and the role of the interpreter in court	152
12	Working paper on access to justice for Deaf people	168

Index	217

PREFACE

The campaign for real interpreting
Graham H. Turner and Frank J. Harrington

Introduction

Interpreting, as an activity, centres around people's desire not to be misunderstood. It is our hope that this book will also not be misunderstood. We have collected these papers together not to produce a dramatic, groundbreaking new theory of interpreting, nor to review the field. This is not a text book; and, whilst the material presented here has in large measure been developed in conjunction with research activity in which we've been involved, this book is not a research report in itself. Instead, bringing these texts together provides a recapitulation of many of the major elements of thinking that have informed our approach to interpreting. In the work presented here, we are trying to understand the nature of the phenomenon, its place in society, and some of the principles which underlie good practice.

Below, we introduce something of our approach to the subject of interpreting. Firstly, though, a word about the papers that follow. This book includes material drawn from sources that date back across a decade (first publication details are listed in an appendix). The texts presented here have not been revised or re-written to take into account the passing of time and they therefore carry a certain amount of historical baggage. Minor changes have been made only in order to reduce distractions to the twenty-first century reader. In most cases, these papers have been published previously, using a wide variety of outlets. This range of original sources was one of the initial reasons for producing this collection: it seemed to us unlikely that any individual would have been able to locate and use all of these texts, given their wide dispersal in the literature. In addition, some of these papers feature unpublished material presented at conferences and workshops but never previously fixed in print.

Given this variable history, plus the range of contributors, it is inevitable that this collection does show its roots. This is not a book with a beginning, a middle and an end, but one in which each paper makes its own independent contribution and can be read in isolation from the others (this is the reason for any elements of repetition). In some respects, too, our own thinking as authors has moved on and we would not necessarily put forward the same arguments or draw the same conclusions were we writing these pieces today—which we consider entirely legitimate and reasonable. But we have resisted the temptation to re-write history and hope that where we've been wrong, we've at least managed to be wrong in interesting or illuminating ways.

Finally, we have also not made this an opportunity to re-cast some of our more overtly anglocentric comments in order to accommodate broader international horizons. We do believe that there are issues here which colleagues working in both signed and spoken language interpreting around the world may find of some interest, and they are well-placed to identify which parts of this volume resonate with their own current concerns. Having offered this apologia, let us continue with a peculiarly English point of departure.

A profession of individuals

For those of a particular cast of mind, one of the finest moments in the world of movies comes during the film *Life of Brian*. The late, great Graham Chapman—playing Brian, a young man born in a stable who has been mistaken for the Messiah—wakes one morning and, naked as the day that he was born, flings open the full-length shutters of his room to find a vast crowd of followers gathered in the square below. They cheer and call on him to speak unto them. His mother tells them to

—'Clear off! He's not the Messiah, he's just a very naughty boy.'

But they will not be budged, and speaking with one voice, ask Brian to tell them his bidding, tell them what they should do. Brian is exasperated: he argues that they don't need anyone to tell them what to do. Rather, his view is that they have to learn to think for themselves.

—'You're all individuals!' he shouts.

—'Yes!', they reply as one, 'We're all individuals!'

There is a perfect hairsbreadth pause.

—'I'm not!' pipes up one small voice.

If there is a thread running through this book, it is perhaps most strongly identifiable in the attempt to put the people—individuals, their inter-relationships and interactions—back into interpreting. Our experience is that many trainee interpreters (probably just like many other kinds of trainees) enter training hoping to be provided with *The Answer*, the fix, the nifty little gadget or one-size-fits-all guiding principle that will make all of their professional dreams come true and every utterance emerge from their mouths perfectly-formed and just as required to further dialogue. For preference, they don't really want the details and the caveats: they want the key to the Kingdom of Interpreter Salvation. Everything we've been told by colleagues working in sign language interpreting overseas, and by spoken language interpreters too, suggests that this is a very commmon experience.

Our approach (not a startlingly original one: we were exposed to a similar idea in our own studies at Durham University with fine teachers such as Mary Brennan, David Brien, Richard Brown, Clark Denmark, Liz Scot Gibson and Marina McIntire) tries to take students back to first principles about the nature of professional work per se. We consider some of these—concerning the need for high-level training, appropriate remuneration, status and respect, an organised workforce with formal qualifications, and so forth—and conclude that, out of this mix, there are two which really stand up to close scrutiny. A great deal that follows is founded upon the bedrock of these two points.

One of these is that professionalism is less about 'how you got there' or your conditions of service upon arrival, and more about your willingness *to be regulated* in the interests of safeguarding appropriate (ethical) standards of practice. A number of papers in this volume set out parts of the reasoning behind identifying the crucial part played by a *Code of Ethics* (or Practice) in embodying this regulatory function and assuring the principle of *institutionalised altruism* (which fundamentally means asserting that the profession should be organised so that the interests of service users are paramount).

The second factor is the *non-routine* nature of professional work. One of the characteristics that distinguishes professions from other occupations appears to be that, for the professional, it is a realistic truism that 'no two jobs are the same'. (Contrast this with some of the more predictable and repetitive tasks that people are required to do in other occupational spheres.)

The combination of these two factors is indeed powerful and needs to be understood profoundly. If you are a sign language interpreter, the Code is not some kind of all-encompassing flow-diagram which will push you and pull you and press your buttons as if by remote control: 'If she says this, then what you do is that. But if she does this, then you need to anticipate the other.' It is more like a set of cartographic principles which will enable you to make maps to assist your everyday journey through unknown terrain. And it is the non-routine nature of the work which ensures that every day, every encounter, every turn at talk is indeed fundamentally unknown terrain.

Research underpinnings

We focus on these elements because we know, as practitioners and academics, that there is strong evidence to support our claims that they are pivotal. We have sought to engage ourselves with the finest available scholarship to provide underpinning knowledge evidence for this approach, and we have had the good fortune to work with inspirational colleagues in environments where an orientation towards research has been expected and encouraged as part of 'the job'.

We have also been involved in a number of research projects which have allowed us to explore questions about 'what interpreters do' and 'what seems to work' for ourselves. All of these projects have involved extensive fieldwork and the collection of many hours of data on videotape. This means that we have been afforded the rare opportunity to reflect—intensively, collaboratively and over an extended period of time—upon interpreting and its effects. We have been able to spend quality time with the 'consumers' of interpreting services and with many service providers, and this has alerted us to many issues and ideas which we have sought to build into our thinking and our discussions here.

The grey zone

If there is one key message that we have gleaned from this work to date, it is this: above all, we have confirmed for ourselves our own understanding of the interpreter, not as a 'conduit' through whom messages pass (without being in any significant way transformed), but as an active third participant in interaction. Too often, people—including many interpreters—behave as if all they are doing is, as it were, taking a message written down by one person, folding it up, and passing it on to another. Once it's unfolded, the metaphor and the behaviour suggest, the message is exactly as it was before. We take a different view, deriving our reasoning (as set out in the pages of this book and elsewhere) from all that we know by reading about, studying, doing and receiving interpreting. For us, what happens as 'the message' is passed from one to another is a much more complex process of transformation—one which makes the achievement of interpreting infinitely more impressive, but also makes quality interpretation a great deal more complex and rare.

Reaching an understanding of the interpreter's active participation, in this sense, entails accepting a certain paradox. Interpreters have freedom, but they also are bound by obligation. On the one hand, if it is accepted that interpreters do not act as conduits, then of necessity they must engage as communicative participants. They are obliged to make choices. (If you don't find this claim convincing, put yourself in the position of the interpreter faced with conversational partners who are talking or signing at the same time. Re-presenting both people's talk at once is a physical impossibility. You have to choose.) On the other hand, where there is choice, this entails the availability of two or more options, so there must be some element of freedom or agency on the part of the interpreter.

An analogy might be with the notion of accent. It is a fairly common experience that people consider themselves to 'have no accent'—because they take their variety of speech for granted as unmarked or neutral on the basis that everyone in the vicinity speaks as they do. Sometimes it takes a long while to convince people that there is no such thing as 'no accent', just a range of possibilities each of which has its place, is susceptible to description and is distinct in particular respects from the others. Similarly, non-intervention is *au fond* not an option for the interpreter.

Just like Brian of Nazareth's followers looking for *The Answer*, students are usually delighted to treat the familiar conduit model as a warm and trusty blanket. Reassuringly simple and decisive, it circumscribes their role tidily and excuses them from responsibility for accounting for their actions. As one student laughingly put it, "It's like: 'Please sir, it wasn't me—the conduit model made me do it!'"

Our task, as we see it, is to challenge this black-and-white picture of interpreter reality. Interpreting isn't like this—if you're honest, goes the message to practitioners, then however much you cling to the *idea*, you know that you don't *actually* operate in accordance with it in your own practice (and physically, nor could you) and anyway you wouldn't be able to do a very effective job if interpreting *were* like this. We invite students to share the conclusion that there are a million shades of grey between the black and the white, and that the interpreting zone is—necessarily and magnificently—a grey zone!

It will be clear that we draw heavily upon, and want others to share, an appreciation of scholarship and the kind of knowledge that can be generated by systematic observation, analysis and theoretical modelling in the light of wider (social) scientific principles and ideas. Over the years, much interpreter training in England has been led by practitioners. Without engagement with underpinning scholarship, the key resources for teachers are personal experience and anecdote—hugely valuable, but not the whole story, and less able to 'get at' certain kinds of 'knowledge'.

Increasingly, though, institutions have engaged in the pursuit of scholarship, and accessed scholarly communities of practice, allowing the generation of 'knowledge' through research to precede, and underpin, training. In these institutions, there has been engagement with theory and innovation on the part of interpreting tutors and, by extension, the trainee interpreters themselves. Underpinning research has been used to illuminate and critique personal experience and anecdote, with analysis and explanation found in this research leading to a greater, or revised, understanding of the principles being presented, and changes in both knowledge and practice.

Nowhere near the end

Sign language interpreting is not, as yet, terribly well-established as a profession on a national or international scale. The scholarship which we're seeking to ally to the field and to use for analytical and training purposes is a similarly recent development, so it is no secret that there many gaps in the kind of thinking presented here. We fully expect to return to these texts in years to come and find ourselves only too aware of numerous flaws (inconsistencies, unwarranted assumptions, misdiagnoses). But for now, this is what we have to offer, and the feedback we've had from students and colleagues suggests that there may be some useful nuggets tucked away in here.

We have organised the material so that it broadly falls into two parts: firstly, discussion of general principles, issues and ideas which, for us, underpin the form of the sign language interpreting profession in general; and secondly, analyses which tend to be more empirically-based and which focus on particular contexts of service-educational, health, social services and legal—in which interpreting services are delivered. Each paper is independent of the others, but there are undoubtedly some key recurring themes. Among these is the notion that there is 'more to interpreting than the contract'. Done properly, it's a very difficult task. Interpreting is not just about knowing where the job is, turning up, talking the talk for an hour or three, and getting paid. Understanding the complex nature of the task, and the role and place of the interpreter in the complex setting of interpreter-mediated talk, demands that interpreters have access to a wide variety of resources, many of which are only available to them as a result of scholarly activity. Essential to their becoming rounded, competent interpreters is the notion that they must not only have good practical skills, business skills, and the like, but that they know and understand the complexity of the task they perform, and this knowledge and understanding comes from their engagement with reflection and study as well as their experience in the work place.

We therefore tend to look to reinforce the message that interpreting is 'grey all the way'. It is simply not an option, if the job is to be done well, for the interpreter to seek to operate on autopilot. Our aim, to date and in future, is therefore to explore as far as possible the complete range of factors (a 'multidimensional space', not just two or three key elements which will 'trip the switches') which may go into the complex and dynamic equations that guide the interpreter's decision-making.

England, as a nation of beer-drinkers, counts among its national institutions an organisation called CAMRA (the Campaign for Real Ale)—beer-drinking diehards who act as a pressure group to 'hold back the tide of fizzy nonsense which is engulfing our Public Houses' (our gloss on their promotional literature)! What they want is no frills, no fizz, honest-to-goodness ale, brewed and served as nature intended. We ask for something similar; the Campaign for Real Interpreting. We assert that there is no one-size-fits-all formula which will make the tough decisions on behalf of the practitioner. The best that she can do—and, as a principle, it is enough if well applied—is to know her options well and endeavour to select appropriately from among them, according to the prevailing circumstances. With this freedom comes the responsibility to make informed choices—and generating that informedness is of course a never-ending, lifelong process—and to be accountable for them. To the extent that interpreters achieve these goals, we feel that the profession is maturing and spreading its wings…

Acknowledgements

We wish to be very clear in our acknowledgement of the contributions made to papers in this collection by co-authors, colleagues, reviewers and research partners of all kinds. In particular, the authorship of each paper here is made explicit as the book unfolds, but we would like to foreground here the identities of all of the original co-authors—Ros Bramwell, Richard Brown, Jennifer Harris, Maureen Reed, Granville Tate and Caroline Taylor (now Bickerton). In each case, the papers that resulted from these collaborations could not have been produced without the insight, experience and knowledge of each contributor. We offer our sincere thanks to all of these co-authors in full appreciation of the quality of their scholarship and collegiality.

Behind-the-scenes contributions also deserve overt recognition, and in this case it is absolutely certain that this volume would not exist were it not for the publication support offered by Doug McLean and Lyn Atkinson. The production process has been assisted greatly by Ernst Thoutenhoofd. Colleagues at the University of Central Lancashire have been instrumental both in developing the thinking embodied here and in creating the time to see this volume through to publication. We are very grateful to them all.

FOREWORD
Marina L. McIntire

What flattery to be asked to write an introduction to this volume! This book will be a real contribution to our field, and I am pleased to attach my name to it. We as a profession have suffered greatly from a serious dearth of academic contributions to our growth. We need academic and theoretical literature which will help us find our place in those circles where decisions are made about funding, curriculum, and program policies. A volume such as this one helps fill that need.

Perhaps more significantly, working interpreters need reassurance about, assistance in, and validation of their work; this is just the sort of book that can provide it. Most of us work alone, without the benefit of collegial support. Facing the sort of ethical dilemmas that we often do, and knowing that we are often facing situations at least somewhat beyond our competence, we need some external help. A book like this can provide just such assistance.

These articles could not have been written or even cobbled together in the years when the profession was forming, for the simple reason that interpreters were too busy inventing ourselves to write things down. I have a colleague who calls us by our 'generations'; perhaps 'wave' is more appropriate. The first wave of interpreters in the US began taking shape in the late 1960's and early 70's. At this time, legal and educational opportunities and privileges for Deaf people were being established and expanded. Suddenly a need for more interpreters was felt and training programs were begun. Initially, six weeks to six months appeared to be a sufficient amount of time to take raw beginners and make them work-ready. (I myself was part of this first wave: I was sent to interpret in university classes precisely ten months after I learned my first sign!)

Soon enough, we realized that more time, training, and education were needed and that perhaps a two-year program would be adequate. Just such programs appeared mushroom-like around the country and many are still functioning in post-secondary, non-university (community) colleges. These two-year programs produced the second wave of interpreters: these people had the advantage of a bit more knowledge of sign language and Deaf people and a bit more time to digest the notion of interpreting. Yet they did not have the language skills, the educational background, nor the maturity in many instances that are required for superior interpreting abilities. Many of us were convinced that four-, even six-year programs would produce something more like what we needed, and as a result, several degree programs, including one graduate-level program, have been established in the US. The third wave of interpreters is now graduating from these and from the better two-year programs which have transformed themselves into three years' worth of education. I would characterize this third wave of interpreters as savvy, relatively well-educated, and more likely to be inclined to a professional approach to the task of working with Deaf people.

Because of Britain's very different educational structures and because of the different history of interpretation in England and Scotland, I do not wish to draw too strong a parallel with the US experience. I believe, however, that our experiences on either side of the Atlantic are not wildly different and that Harrington and Turner's work represents the best of this third wave of interpreters in Britain. They have produced for us here some thoughtful and even radical discussions of the profession and practice of signed language interpretation. These are probably not the 'last word' in our development; they are, however, the latest word from the front, where interpreters are working and where students are being taught to interpret.

I salute the authors on their achievements, which are impressive to say the least, and I salute the coming fourth wave of interpreters in our field. You will have every advantage over those who have come before. We can only hope that this will reflect in increased opportunities and better services for Deaf people, both in the UK and around the world.

Marina L. McIntire
Lecturer, Department of Anthropology, California State University, and Interpreter, National Center on Deafness

FOREWORD
'One World?'
Franz Pöchhacker

It may seem presumptuous for a conference interpreter who remained largely ignorant of sign language interpreting well past completion of his Ph.D. in interpreting studies to write a preface to a book on that topic. Indeed, my record as an author on interpreting suggests that what I could hope to contribute here is, at best, an outsider's perspective on sign language (SL) interpreting issues. Whatever the merits of this point-of-view, it would at least be representative of the prevailing position within what one might call the mainstream of interpreting studies as an emerging academic discipline. In fact, however, I would like to address the readership of this collection of papers on SL interpreting from an integrationist perspective, as a spokesman for the view that the systematic study of interpreting needs to be based on a concept of 'interpreting' that is not *a priori* blind or indifferent to some of its more relevant features.

Such a 'one-world' approach to interpreting studies implies that the papers collected in this volume are relevant not only to those dealing with interpreting with Deaf people but also—and certainly no less—to those investigating interpreting in other modalities. For one, the well-established paradigm of 'conference interpreting research', which shares with SL interpreting the predominance of the simultaneous mode, is increasingly giving serious attention to interpreting as a 'service' to meet the needs and expectations of various users. Since scholars of SL interpreting have long been aware of—and focused their analytical interest on—the crucial relationship between interpreters and their clients, papers on this topic, like the ones included in this volume, promise interesting insights for anyone looking beyond (simultaneous) interpreting as a cognitive processing task.

The same holds true for other domains of interpreting which are often viewed as special applications of conference interpreting skills, like media interpreting and court interpreting. Nevertheless, despite sporadic claims by the International Association of Conference Interpreters, the work of interpreters in the (national) courtroom stands little chance of being governed by the comfortable standards of practice established for international settings. Rather, (spoken-language) court interpreting in many countries remains underdeveloped both in terms of professional standards and as an object of in-depth research. What efforts have been made in this regard (and these have indeed been considerable over the past decade or so), have generally been made without the benefit of systematic cooperation with court interpreters working with Deaf people. The analyses provided in this volume may well enhance the level of cooperation among scholars of court interpreting in any modality and provide valuable insights into the workings of specific institutional constraints and their impact on interpreters and their clients.

Leaving aside the controversy over the conceptual status of court interpreting as a sub-domain of 'community interpreting' or else a field of professional practice in its own right, there is no doubt that the emerging 'discipline' of community interpreting is the one with the most obvious links and interfaces with the study of SL interpreting. While the landmark conferences on this topic (the Canadian 'Critical Link' series) have made a point of incorporating the concerns of SL interpreting, most efforts aimed at professionalizing and investigating interpreting in community settings, such as the work of the European Association BABELEA, remain focused on the spoken modality, with many researchers denying themselves the benefit of learning from those who have been at the forefront of moves to enhance the professional practice and scientific study of interpreting in the community. Indeed, as regards one of the dominant research issues—the complexity of the interpreter's role in the triadic constellation—scholars of (spoken-language) community interpreting can hardly expect much guidance and inspiration from their well-established colleagues in the field of conference interpreting; rather, it is SL interpreters and SL interpreting researchers who represent the cutting edge in the drive towards conceptualizing the interpreter's role and putting codes of practice and ethics to the test by means of innovative empirical investigations. While the specific national, cultural and institutional contexts will of course differ, the diversity of settings should not detract from the possibility of taking a more united analytical approach to the complex socio-psychological research problems posed by our object of study.

In short, there are good reasons for many interpreting scholars in the various sub-areas of the discipline to take a closer look at research on SL interpreting such as the work by Graham Turner and Frank Harrington and associates collected in this volume. In light of the 'one-world' approach advocated above it seems fitting that I should have met Graham Turner at a conference in Dublin entitled Unity in Diversity. In my contribution to that event—an exploratory analysis of bibliographical cross-referencing between conference, community and SL interpreting research—my findings for the state of unity in diversity in interpreting studies had been rather sobering. Some five years later, the prospects for closer integration seem better than ever, and the present volume should prove invaluable for an intensified exchange between the sub-communities of what I regard as 'our world' of interpreting studies.

Franz Pöchhacker
Associate Professor, Department of Translation & Interpreting,
University of Vienna

1
REFLECTIONS ON CONSTRUCTING AN INTERPRETING PROFESSION

Rights and responsibilities:
the relationship between Deaf people and interpreters
Graham H. Turner

Introduction

In this, the first part of a two-part article, I examine the relationship between interpreters and Deaf people, focusing on the rights and responsibilities that belong to Deaf people within this somewhat interdependent relationship. In part two (*Regulation and responsibility: the relationship between interpreters and Deaf people*—this volume), I look more closely at interpreters and the development of a mutually supportive, constructively critical relationship between professional service providers and consumers. Readers may find it odd that a hearing person who is not an interpreter should be writing on this issue. The article should certainly be considered with this in mind. At the same time, it may be seen as valuable to have a relatively disinterested commentary on such sensitive matters. My primary aim is simply to stimulate discussion.

New Deaf times

In case you hadn't noticed, it's been 'all-change' lately at the top of the Deaf community in the UK. The result carries at least some interesting echoes of the current position at the top in the wider community. At the BDA, we now have the energetic young figure of Jeff McWhinney, leading the UK's main democratic, membership-led Deaf organisation in the vital activities of campaigning and political lobbying. Who is his equal in the wider community? Surely Tony Blair fits the bill well—the new, energetic young leader of the Labour Party, the main democratic, membership-led organisation in the UK's wider political framework?

And at the RNID—the vast (and vastly wealthy) service-providing, 'quality-assuring' institution, with its City-and-corporate ethos and its coveted position as an 'establishment' organisation—we now have the honourable pin-striped politico, Doug Alker. And *his* hearing alter ego? Well, given the state of British politics—with the Conservative Party engaged in a leadership election even as I write—I had better not state the analogy that I originally had in mind here, since it may well be way past its sell-by date by the time you come to be reading these words! I'll give you a clue, though: it wasn't Margaret Thatcher!

I say all of this, of course, with my tongue very firmly in my cheek and I'm sure the gentlemen in question will take it in the appropriate spirit. I dare say that Mr McWhinney has also been seen in wide Wall Street braces and I know (see 'Influences', *New Statesman & Society*, 10 February 1995, page 30) that Mr Alker considers some of his major influences to have been not-exactly-right-wing figures such as Thomas Paine. Nevertheless, it surely isn't too far-fetched to see the RNID and the BDA as rather neat ciphers for the Conservative and Labour parties, and so to consider the Deaf political scene as a microcosm of the wider national picture. Where does such a comparison lead?

Two Deaf agendas

Doug Alker's arrival as the first Deaf Chief Executive of the RNID may have led to two-and-three-quarter cheers (investors are reminded that share values may fall as well as rise), but there has been no suggestion that any kind of dramatic changes are afoot within the Institute beyond a long overdue move from the labyrinthine premises at 105 Gower Street. Mr Alker has been at pains to stress (see 'New chief sends out the right signals', *The Independent*, 19 January 1995) that the BSL-using Deaf community should expect no special favours and that it will be essentially 'business as usual' as the RNID caters for its consumer base of some 8,000,000 people, of whom the 50,000 BSL-users constitute only a tiny minority.

The very terminology which now trips from the fingertips when people—including insiders—discuss the RNID seems to me in itself to be indicative of the direction of the prevailing winds in the Gower Street region. 'Business as usual' catches the mood because it is exactly as a business-like enterprise that the RNID now appears overwhelmingly to see itself. It has, during the present period of Conservative domination of the political scene, reinvented itself with great aplomb in line with the market-forces rhetoric and sharp PR image-making of these still Thatcherite times. Crucially, it has also successfully realigned itself in relation to its constituency: these are now consumers to whom the RNID provides a service as efficiently and cost-effectively as it possibly can.

What is one to say? It is indisputably true that the RNID has, for instance, set up and staffed a quite astonishing number of Communication Support Units across these isles in an extremely short space of time, and that large numbers of Deaf people are able to avail themselves of the services they provide. This is not a negligible achievement, and it is matched (though not necessarily so dramatically) by the Institute in other areas of service provision. The Units are kept staffed with personnel who are largely trained and supervised in-house by the RNID. Administrative costs are kept competitively low, and I understand that members of the public are even able to book interpreters using no-charge 0800 telephone numbers. They've thought of everything, you might say.

Here, then, we have the first 'Deaf agenda'. It is certainly markedly different to the historical perception that Deaf people were unfortunate folk who needed special help and extra support. Deaf people, the RNID approach says, in fact need only to be offered quality services in a professional manner, and they will exercise their purchasing power as consumers to buy the services they choose to use.

The party opposite

Whatever the RNID's size and weight, the BDA can still claim to be the real representative organisation of BSL-using Deaf people, having gone through its own 'one member, one vote' constitutional shift and having now *pro-actively* appointed its first Deaf leader, Jeff McWhinney. The real point of the comparison with Tony Blair that I made above was to allude to the idea that the BDA, and Mr McWhinney in particular, might find it constructive to see if there are any leaves in the Labour Party book that could usefully be faxed up to Carlisle for a Deaf re-write. If the RNID can recognise its own polished ethos gleaming out from 10 Downing Street, and can make such phenomenal political and economic capital from doing so, then perhaps the relatively rough-hewn BDA can see far enough into the future to imagine a time when the Blairite tendency may gain the upper hand at the request of the electorate. Perhaps the Deaf community would welcome the chance to signify similar preferences.

Do I have anything particular in mind? Funny you should ask. It just so happens that I do.

Consider this. What ideological stance is the Labour Party currently forging for itself? A number of distinguished political commentators have noted that the more the Tory government pushes through the agenda of change instigated by Margaret Thatcher, the more traditional values wind up in the ideological lost property box. Anthony Giddens (1994:38) has argued that as a result of "foot-shuffling, yet dogged, worship of market forces ... the route back to one-nation Toryism is blocked. For one-nation conservatism depended upon forms of tradition, deference and habit that free market conservatism has helped to undermine". The Labour Party, Giddens continues, has begun to respond by looking to claim that lost property: "Let's—it might be said—oppose the New Right capitulation to the market, let's recreate communities, and let's stress duties and obligations, rather than following the usual leftist preoccupation with rights. I would say this is more or less the position Tony Blair has got to..." (1994:38).

I would like to suggest that the Deaf community, too, often appears to be focused upon the "usual leftist preoccupation with rights". In the current political climate—sadly, it is no longer 1968, and the slogan 'Be realistic: demand the impossible' cuts little ice—this has to be recognised as a risky strategy. If it is, then the same kind of "radical critique" that Paul Gilroy urged upon Black people in the UK five years ago—advocating a reigning in of the moralistic excesses practised in the name of anti-racism (Gilroy, 1990)—seems wholly applicable here. In 1991, Jeff McWhinney himself was making connections between the oppression of Deaf people and that experienced by Black people (McWhinney 1991). I look to him to continue to make those connections, updating them and maintaining the same politically pragmatic moderation which he advocated at that time.

What might the Deaf equivalent of Gilroy's "radical critique" be? For racist, read 'audist'. The audist establishment (Lane 1992) that for so long kept Deaf people out of the driving seat of their own lives has some deep and cherished roots. The anti-audist, rights-claiming orthodoxy has doubtless made tremendous progress on behalf of all Deaf people, but it has also in turn become a target of critique in an anti-anti-audist backlash (see, for instance, Stewart, 1992 and Bertling, 1994). So the argument I advance is essentially pragmatic. It is intended to head off that backlash at the pass. Let's be clear: there is, in my view, no denying the validity of the claim to rights. I am pressing the belief that the claim to rights will be greeted more favourably when it is coupled with a parallel acceptance of a concomitant set of responsibilities.

It is widely acknowledged that the 'guru' of the rights-and-responsibilities approach is Amitai Etzioni. Etzioni's book *The Spirit of Community* consolidates a set of ideas which have become known as 'communitarianism'. One element of the communitarian approach is the presentation of the moral position that rights must, in all justice, be matched by responsibilities. Etzioni emphasises that whilst we do have the political and economic right to make demands on our fellow citizens, we also have duties to others (Anderson and Davey 1995a).

Of course, one must recognise that what is being presented is no matter of mere legislation: "Etzioni demands nothing less than a transformation of the way people behave. Put simply, we must all embrace our responsibilities without coercion. The only incentive is that it is right to do so" (Anderson and Davey 1995b:21). This desire for a transformation of behaviour is precisely the one I would commend to Mr McWhinney. I urge him to see that the case for Deaf advancement which he will be arguing in his post at the BDA will be immeasurably strengthened in the eyes of the wider community if he can lead the Deaf membership of the BDA to a stronger and more substantial sense of their place as socially responsible citizens *even as* he continues to make known the undeniable ethical arguments against the widespread oppression of Deaf people.

Rights, responsibilities and interpreting

I promised in the introduction to this piece to focus on matters arising in the provision of interpreting services used by Deaf people. My thoughts were forcibly kickstarted at the recent 2nd National Meeting of Sign Language Interpreting Agencies, a one-day session for discussion of current practices in the field, organised by the Council for the

Advancement of Communication with Deaf People (CACDP). The tone for that day was strikingly set by CACDP Chief Executive, Stewart Simpson, who asserted (Simpson 1995) that many in the field were now of the opinion that there remained no "joy" in our work.

I tend to be of the opinion that the source of the 'joy drought', as it were, is not terribly hard to spot. The advances made in the cause of social justice for Deaf people in the UK largely came clinging to the (lengthy, transatlantic) coat-tails of Martin Luther King. At the time, the weight of moral arguments for civil rights was evidently considered overwhelming and self-sufficient. For these rights, however, the writing was surely on the wall by the time we were faced with the specious, short-sighted logic of Thatcher/Reagan 'good housekeeping' policies in the 'enterprise culture' of the 1980s. Perhaps Stewart Simpson's joy met its nemesis with the recent arrival to high office in the USA of Newt Gingrich's Republicanism. Our world faces the inexorable approach of the day when some under-Newt concludes in tub-thumping tones that "the experiment in social justice simply has not paid off. In other words, the Deaf contribution to GNP has never been greater than the capital outlay on plant and infrastructure. The policy can therefore no longer be seen to be economically sustainable". Don't forget, you read it here first, folks. Where has the joy gone? It went up in a puff of smoke lit by a torch fueled with 'bottom lines' and 'profitable returns upon our advance'.

The mood of the CACDP meeting, one which I share, was—I think—that the key to the renaissance of joy (or at least a little quiet satisfaction) must lie in the development of a mutually respectful relationship between interpreters and Deaf people. The notion that the fortunes of these groups of people are to an extent interdependent is not new (see, for example, Pollitt 1991). But the idea that it may be constructive for both sides to see this relationship in terms of rights and corresponding responsibilities has a particularly contemporary flavour.

Four angles on responsibility
First angle

I would like to outline four instances of the kind of responsibility I have in mind. I focus on this side of the rights–responsibilities equation on the assumption that readers of this article are already more than familiar with the argumentation in favour of Deaf people's rights. I have written elsewhere (Turner 1994a, 1994b) of the sense that the most extreme pro-Deaf arguments—pressed home in the 1970s and 1980s at a time when the weight of oppressive, medico-pathological inertia needed to be aggressively thrown off—are now due for reappraisal in the light of contemporary understandings of Deaf socio-cultural positions. The acceptance of the responsibilities that correspond to Deaf rights could be a constructive element within such a reappraisal.

Firstly, at a time when bodies such as CACDP, the Association of Sign Language Interpreters (ASLI) and the Scottish Association of Sign Language Interpreters (SASLI) continue to campaign for recognition of the professional status of BSL/English interpreters, it seems to me appropriate to look to Deaf people themselves to share the responsibility for promoting the use of interpreters who are adequately educated and regulated and who can be held professionally accountable for their work as interactional mediators. Of course there are some unqualified persons who can do a good job of individual interpreting assignments; just as, in a recent cause célèbre, no-one doubts that the hospital porter who assisted in the theatre during a surgical procedure (an amputation, as I recall) made a perfectly adequate contribution to the success of the operation. Such instances notwithstanding, in the longer term surely the way to achieve consistency, control and a secure assurance of quality is through the deployment of a conscientious, professional workforce. The right to an interpreter whose work on your behalf may be liable to cause you nothing but trauma and distress is no right at all.

I would argue that, in this respect, Deaf people are no different to other members of our society. Even if all of the people present at some institutional event (in education, local government, medicine, the law and so on) declare a preference for the unqualified interpreter, don't we—as citizens with some stake in the outcome of the interaction—all have a responsibility to settle only for the regulated, professional alternative? To take one example, when a BSL/English interpreter appears in a police station, their responsibility does not stop with those persons present in the room. Especially in public institutions, you and I as fellow citizens also have a vested interest in seeing the job effectively and humanely done. In 1990s Britain, 'humaneness' seems often to be considered an irrelevance, but if one recasts the point in terms of taxpayers' pounds—e.g. the cost of police and subsequent judicial attention—possibly being wasted while first someone misinterprets and later the effect of the misinterpretation is mitigated, it seems to hit home. What I'm suggesting, therefore, is that Deaf people as responsible citizens owe it to themselves and to others to contribute to the development of properly professional interpreting services by choosing, where possible, to *use* such services.

Second angle

A second element of the responsibility side of the equation was also raised at the CACDP Agencies Meeting, this time by Albert Thomson, CACDP Development Officer for BSL (Thomson 1995). Thomson discussed in particular the role of Deaf people within the management structures of sign language interpreting agencies. Among the conclusions emerging from the discussion was the perception that individual Deaf people may require some form of training before being able to fulfil their management remit as effectively as possible. Managerial boards, it was argued, certainly need Deaf input, but there could be gaps between the input given and the views of the community as a whole. In other words, those undertaking such managerial roles were not necessarily finding ways adequately to *represent* the constituency on whose behalf they were expected to report.

Again, I suggest that this can be seen as a clear rights-and-responsibilities issue. It appears to be uncontroversial that Deaf users of interpreting services do have a right to make their views about those services known to administrators, managers and other senior figures. However, I would venture that in tandem with this right, those given the task of reporting to the board must be expected to take very seriously indeed their responsibility to present any concerns in a manner that is an accurate reflection of the views of the consumer group. The alternative is not only less than satisfactory but also less than just.

Third angle

For the third angle, I turn to yet another paper from the same CACDP meeting (congratulations are in order to CACDP, it seems, for what was certainly a stimulating day's proceedings). In his paper (Harrington 1995) at the meeting, Frank Harrington raised as a potential issue for consideration the prospect of Deaf people receiving monies under the Disability Living Allowance (DLA) scheme as a result of their social communicative needs. Why should this pose any problems? As Harrington acknowledged, it may be somewhat pessimistic to foresee any difficulties—it is understood at the time of writing that a further Government appeal is being planned against the relevant Court of Appeal decision in the case of Becky Halliday (made on the 15th June 1995)—but the repercussions certainly *could* squarely juxtapose Deaf people's rights against their responsibilities.

DLA is a grant to be used at the recipient's discretion and Harrington speculates that some Deaf people "might use it for other things more important to them than interpreting services". Meanwhile, however, corporate funding to bodies like interpreting agencies (such as that from Local Authorities) is liable to be cut—the logic being "well, if DLA is giving Deaf people the power to buy their own personal interpreting service as and when they need it, then it makes no sense for us to put forward financial support for exactly the same service". Should both of these things happen, Harrington points out, the net result will be a major drop in funding for sign language interpreting services used by members of the Deaf community. Harrington concludes: "If corporate funding were to disappear because of this, the future of interpreting services would be quite literally in the hands of the Deaf community."

This too, it seems to me, is a classic rights-and-responsibilities scenario. Deaf people would have a *right* to the money that would bring them purchasing power, and a corresponding *responsibility* to consider fully the ways in which that financial muscle should be flexed.

Fourth angle

Finally, and perhaps most controversially, what of the expectations which Deaf people have about their direct inter-relations with interpreters? It appears increasingly to be the case that the profile of the interpreting cadre is younger and that these persons do not have Deaf families but have entered the field on a more-or-less purely occupational basis. Are these young professionals well-prepared for the climate that will face them? This may be a hard one to call, but it does seem to be the case that the burn-out rate amongst those entering this field is growing ever more rapid. Discussions in international fora show that this is by no means a phenomenon specific to these isles.

What point do we reach if we follow this line? One can, arguably, envisage that we get a scene dominated by persons who are less inclined to maintain present ideas of professionalism (since these may be seen as somehow behind the burn-out explosion). The prospect of a field dominated by unprofessional, unconscientious and/or disempowering interpreters is surely less than appealing. What possible responsibility could Deaf people have to prevent this scenario becoming a reality?

Well, why do interpreters 'burn out'? It is unlikely that any single cause would ever be responsible. An accumulation of frustrations and difficulties is perhaps more to be expected. In my limited experience, one of the many reasons can be the unrealistic expectations that some Deaf people have of them (which is not *by any means* to say that other people don't have false expectations too). Let me try to give one example. There is of course much to be said for interpreters having social as well as professional contact with the communities in which they work: awareness of current trends and issues is extremely important. However, don't Deaf people also have a responsibility to recognise that there must—it is in everyone's interests that there *should*—be limits to that relationship? The vast majority of interpreters are *not* Deaf people, and both their professional and personal selves need to have the space to maintain a sense of their own identity and individuality, especially when they spend huge chunks of their waking hours taking on other personas and trying to get inside other people's skin in order to do their job properly as interpersonal mediators.

There are many instances, it seems to me, when Deaf people—whatever their fundamental understanding of these issues—in practice do not act upon their knowledge of such a responsibility. To take but one hypothetical example, if a meeting is held in which interpreters and Deaf people come together outside the working day to discuss matters of common concern, what language or languages will the meeting be conducted in? I know of more than one occasion when either interpreters have been angered by Deaf participants' insistance that the interpreters sign, or Deaf people have been angered by the interpreters' insistence that they will use speech and have this interpreted by a third party. I am willing to bet that some Deaf people reading this now will feel that speech would be an inappropriate or even oppressive choice by the hearing people. This is why I believe we have a rights and responsibilities issue here: many Deaf people know about their right to access, but do not see that there is a responsibility also to uphold the interpreters' parallel right to self-expression.

I suggest that that example gives, in microcosm, a sense of a much broader situation. It is a situation in which interpreters are liable to burn out at least partly because the responsibility to acknowledge *their* rights is not always accepted.

Always two sides

No matter how thin you make the pancake, as they say, there are always two sides. It will be clear to all that I have presented a very one-sided story here, and I make no apology for this. I have already promised a second part to this discussion which will, in its way, turn the topic on its head and ask questions of the interpreting profession. I don't pretend to be speaking for anyone else but myself in all of the above, and those with more first-hand knowledge may well feel that there are glaring gaps in the argument. I am, of course, quite happy that these gaps be filled. I'd be delighted to see the questions I've raised and the challenges I've implicitly posed addressed, especially by Deaf people, in future. There is much ground to cover.

Acknowledgements

Thanks are due especially to Kyra Pollitt, and also to Mary Brennan, Richard Brown, Frank Harrington and Maureen Reed for comments made in the preparation of this paper. They nevertheless bear no responsibility for the final text.

References

Anderson, P. and Davey, K. (1995a) Import duties. *New Statesman and Society*, 8/342: 18–20.

—— (1995b) Tough on crime. New Statesman and Society, 8/342:21.

Bertling, T. (1994) *A Child Sacrificed to the Deaf Culture*. Kodiak Media Group: Wilsonville, OR.

Giddens, A. (1994) What's Left for Labour? *New Statesman and Society*, 7/322:37–40.

Gilroy, P. (1990) The end of antiracism. In Ball, W. and Solomos, J. (eds) *Race and Local Politics*. Macmillan Publishers: London.

Harrington, F. (1995) Funding issues for agencies. CACDP 2nd National Meeting of Sign Language Interpreting Agencies. London, 4 April 1995.

Lane, H. (1992) *The Mask of Benevolence*. Alfred A. Knopf: New York, NY.

McWhinney, J. (1991) Deaf consciousness. *Signpost*, 4/1:13–15.

Pollitt, K. (1991) Rational responses. *Signpost*, 4/2: 24.

Simpson, S. (1995) If I was going there, I wouldn't start from here. CACDP 2nd National Meeting of Sign Language Interpreting Agencies. London, 4 April 1995.

Stewart, L. (1992) Debunking the Bilingual/Bicultural Snow Job in the American Deaf Community. In Garretson, M. (ed) *Viewpoints on Deafness*. Gallaudet University Press: Washington, DC.

Thomson, A. (1995) The role of Deaf people in the development of Sign Language Interpreting Agencies. CACDP 2nd National Meeting of Sign Language Interpreting Agencies. London, 4 April 1995.

Turner, G. H. (1994a) How is Deaf culture? *Sign Language Studies*, 83. 103–126.

—— (1994b) Response to Bahan, Montgomery, Ladd and Further Discussion. *Sign Language Studies*, 85. 337–366.

Regulation and responsibility: the relationship between interpreters and Deaf people
Graham H. Turner

Introduction

In the first part of this two-part article, I examined the relationship between interpreters and Deaf people, focusing on some of the rights and responsibilities that can be seen to belong to Deaf people themselves within this somewhat interdependent communion. I suggested that the arrival of new Deaf Chief Executives at the Royal National Institute for Deaf People (RNID) and British Deaf Association (BDA) gave a valuable opportunity for reflection upon the way forward with regard to views of the interpreting profession. I should repeat that readers may find it odd that a hearing person who is not an interpreter should be writing on this issue, and the analysis I offer should certainly be considered with this in mind. At the same time, it may be seen as valuable to have a relatively disinterested commentary on what are inevitably sensitive matters. My primary aim is simply to stimulate discussion: I'm sure readers will be quite happy to come to their own conclusions about how insightful, or otherwise, these comments are.

Whilst the interpreting profession can still fairly be described as 'emerging' (as it was by Liz Scott Gibson in 1991), it has long been clear that what will emerge is going to depend to a considerable extent upon the development of a mutually supportive, though constructively critical, relationship between service providers and consumers (Pollitt, 1991). I argued in the earlier paper that although Deaf people do have a right to quality interpreting, they also have the responsibility not to take features of that service for granted. In the second part of this article, I shall turn that perspective on its head to take a look at the corresponding contribution that interpreters themselves might be asked to make to the provider-consumer relationship.

Responsibility and professionalism in the Nineties

What views do interpreters currently hold about their relationship with Deaf consumers of their services? Two kinds of comments frequently strike me when I talk to interpreters. On the one hand, interpreters frequently discuss their working practices in ways that show the considerable extent to which they *are* concerned to support Deaf consumers. On the other, it is striking that interpreters take pains to defer, across a whole range of issues, to the directions enshrined in the Council for the Advancement of Deaf People (CACDP) and Scottish Association of Sign Language Interpreters (SASLI) Codes of Practice/Ethics. Many people state that their response to interpreting dilemmas is effectively conditioned by what 'the interpreting role' is and is not. People are concerned to know and feel confident about what *exactly* their role does and does not 'permit' them to do, and they look to these Codes, in many instances, for *instructions* about what they may do.

I would like to look further at the two elements identified above. Both, I suggest, in fact relate to the question, 'What do interpreters understand the notion of professionalism to mean to them?' This is a matter I take up in full recognition that it is part, at least, of the umbrella question with which I faced myself some years ago: "How can interpreters be made more wisely powerful and enabled to take on the burden of their responsibilities with confidence and care?" (Turner 1991:19).

We live in an age of considerable tension in many occupational fields. A great deal of this tension arises as a result of recent changes in the organisation and operation of working practices. The principal driving force behind such changes has been central government, which—under Margaret Thatcher and her successor John Major—carefully overturned what it considered to be unconstructively tight controls on employment and working practices. It has taken the deregulation of business and occupational conditions to be one of its big ideas to take Britain into the 21st century.

In following such a programme, the government has no shortage of influential supporters. The Institute of Directors made its own case for deregulation in *Controlled in Everything* (1992, cited by Lashmar 1994). The recommendations therein included the abolition of licences for activities ranging from driving lessons and tattooing to keeping a bull as a semen donor. The Institute makes clear that it feels Britain's working practices are subjected to an unhelpful—and even possibly damaging—level of monitoring. There are too many checks and balances, it is claimed, which ultimately serve to reduce the value of services and commercial activities by setting up far too many hoops for suppliers and providers to jump through.

Of course, a sector tightly-regulated on paper would not be likely to operate as such in practice without enforcement. But, again, cutbacks mean that the personnel that would be required for thorough enforcement of regulations simply do not exist in many fields. The *Yorkshire Evening Post* of 26 February 1994, for instance, reported that bus firms were breaking regulations because the Department of Transport could not afford to monitor them. Apparently we can no longer afford to be independently assured of our safety or feel secure with the quality of goods and services provided to us.

Living in interesting times

And so, as regards the regulation of working practices, we certainly seem to live in interesting times. A parallel—and, doubtless, related—development has been the steady dissolution in modern times of the notion of professionalism. The same kind of array of checks and balances, tests and substantial quality assurance assessments that once constituted the regulator's armoury also feature in public understandings of what professionalism entails. The rationalised, route one, if-no-one-complains-it-must-be-okay society of 1990s Britain seems to have correspondingly little time for the arguments that quality of service can only be certain when highly-trained, knowledgeable, ethically guided, self-directed and appropriately-paid service providers are employed. But does the notion of professionalism capture anything worth saving anyway?

It is not difficult for people to trot out exhortations to interpreters, as to other workers, to 'be professional': indeed, many Codes of Practice/Ethics do so. Nor is it uncommon to read things like the following in the interpreting literature: "If you want to be taken for a professional, you must behave like a professional—and your work should come up to professional standards" (Katschinka 1988:120). And there are now a number of accounts available that describe interpretation between a signed and a spoken language as an 'emerging' profession (Fenton 1993, Scott Gibson 1990). But the notion of professionalism is not unproblematic.

During the second half of the 20th century, it has largely been received wisdom that professions could be set apart from other occupations by virtue of a set of identifying traits or attributes (see, for example, Hoyle 1980) that showed how the profession had, in effect, struck a bargain with society. Expert knowledge gave professionals power over clients, but the professional was "assigned a reasonable, even generous, level of status and material rewards in return for an undertaking of non-exploitation (the presence of an ethical code), the maintenance of standards of training and qualification and other guarantees to society" (Crompton 1990:152). Thus far, we seem to have a picture that fits in regard to the BSL/English interpreting profession.

However, understanding of the meaning of professionalism has moved on. In a carefully argued sociological critique, Crompton reports the polite conclusion that the search for essential professional qualities or attributes was "not particularly successful" (1990:152). For many theorists, the trait approach, after rigourous analysis and refinement, ultimately did no more than uncritically to take on board the professionals' own (idealised) definition of themselves: "Rather than providing a vital service or function for society, professions were seen to be occupations on the make, who had used (and use) their monopoly of knowledge and technique in order to secure their own advantage" (Crompton 1990:153). Again, this is certainly an accusation that is nowadays quite commonly thrown at interpreters. The recent coinage of the signed phrase 'deaf wage', which describes a (hearing) person who takes advantage for their own gain of money made available to support Deaf people (a sign which is more readily applied to interpreters than to members of any other occupational category), is strong evidence of the reality of this opinion within the Deaf community. (I am indebted to Maureen Reed for alerting me to this example.)

Sociological conclusions

A strong case, then, can be made for arguing that the sociological distinction between 'professions' and other skilled and expert occupations "should be finally laid to rest... It may be argued that the 'sociology of the professions' has contributed a number of important insights into the analysis of the regulation of expert knowledge, but 'professionals' should not be regarded as being a distinctive category separate from other experts" (Crompton 1990:156–7).

Parts of the sociologists' analyses lead to the conclusion that—in many ways irrespective of the wrangles over the meaning of the word 'professional'—the sociology of work still offers valuable insights into the tenor of occupational practices of skilled workers like interpreters which we would be wise not to lose sight of. For a start, the 'bargain' struck by the regulated expert labourer of any kind, referred to by Merton (1982:118) as 'institutionalised altruism'—a selfless ethical code in return for considerations of status and reward—retains a certain undeniable resonance especially in situations where clients/employers cannot possibly be responsible for judging the quality of the service supplied.

It has to be noted that, in the context of the somewhat pessimistic discussion above concerning the present 'hands-off' approach to the control and ethical guidance of service and business practices, it seems rather perverse even to discuss moral regulation in a market society. It is to the situation of BSL/English interpreters as regulated expert labourers that I now turn.

Regulation is professionalism?

The thrust of Rosemary Crompton's sociological argument is that the notion of *profession* does not describe a generic occupational type, but a continuingly significant *mode of regulation* of the provision of expert labour, coupled with educational standards that can be used by non-specialists as an informal guarantee of fitness-to-practice. In other words, it is not some set of characteristics of the occupational culture or conditioning that mark out professions from non-professions, but rather the manner in which the work done is monitored and regulated (for those who prefer the contemporary jargon, let us say 'the way in which quality is assured').

The central point of reference for BSL/English interpreters here is their *Code of Practice*/Ethics. The interpreter who abides by, and respects the authority of, the Code 'buys into' the relevant mode of regulation for workers in this field—and can thereby, Crompton would suggest, be legitimately designated 'a professional'. BSL/English interpreters, on the whole, do take their Codes extremely seriously, to the extent of seeing them as the primary codification of their role and responsibilities. And, even in the current climate of deregulation, these expert labourers perceive themselves to have their working practices closely delimited and controlled by the statutes enshrined in the Codes. Their view seems to be that the Code they follow is the conveyor of professional status—if you're trained to do what it says, and you do what it says, then you're being professional.

If this is accepted, then we could argue—quite convincingly, I think—that, given the view that professionalism is about the (ethical) mode of regulation of an occupational group, BSL/English interpreters do in fact *already* constitute a fully professional population rather than an emerging one (to the extent that they adhere to the Code: Manasse (1993:66) intriguingly notes that only half of the respondents to her survey claimed to be fully conversant with the Code).

CACDP and SASLI

One thing is immediately obvious in the light of all that has been said above. The tide in occupational practice—deregulation washing at all our toes—is presently running markedly *against* the desire to strengthen the BSL/English interpreting profession through maximising the potential of the regulatory function of Codes of Practice/Ethics. CACDP has very recently used its own powers to strike off one trainee interpreter from the register (on the grounds of repeated non-appearance for appointments). One gets the impression that this was a step taken with great reluctance, given the ongoing shortage of qualified interpreters. Yet this move has been applauded from within the field, which is a promising sign. It is imperative that CACDP and SASLI as the regulatory bodies are seen to carry out this function with alacrity and robust precision. Anything less will simply serve to undermine the immeasurably powerful assets that have evolved in the shape of the current Codes of Practice/Ethics as interpreted by those they govern. The scope for abuse of the professional capacity and status is broad indeed if CACDP and SASLI show themselves to be too frightened to take their own Codes seriously.

I would like to suggest, taking the above as a useful springboard, that a slight realignment of Merton's concept of 'institutionalised altruism' could constructively modify our understanding of what the professional interpreter should be directed to do (and in many instances, clearly already does). The twist I would like to give would be to talk instead of 'institutionalised responsibility'. For it seems to me that 'altruism' does not truly capture the breadth of the true professional's commitment to the communal goals of his/her endeavour; nor does it seem to match what I believe to be a genuine desire to advance social aims as expressed by so many interpreters. 'Institutionalised responsibility' would cover responsibility (a) to service users, both Deaf and hearing, (b) to the profession, i.e. to colleagues present and future, (c) to the job, i.e. to the integrity of the task, (d) to oneself and (e) to the citizens of the wider society.

This last point seems to me to be crucial. What is being said is that to be a professional means to 'buy into' an occupational culture that insists upon ethical regulation in the interests of all. When a BSL/English interpreter appears in a court of law, for instance, their responsibility does not stop with those members of the public present in the room. In public institutions most clearly (but elsewhere too), society—you and I as fellow citizens—has a vested interest in seeing the job well, effectively, efficiently and humanely done. In 1990s Britain, 'humaneness' seems often to be considered an irrelevance: policy makers having an alarming tendency not to notice if lives are damaged, so long as the job is done cheaply. But if one recasts the point in terms of taxpayers' pounds—the costs of the court's attention, as it might be—being wasted while someone misinterprets, it seems to hit home relatively uncontroversially.

A Profession beyond the Nineties

And so the emerging suggestion is that the nature of the regulation currently in place for BSL/English interpreters (especially if modified to take into account the sense of institutionalised responsibility which is advanced here as a beneficial recasting of our sense of ethically-motivated expert labour), coupled with the knowledge that interpreters are already inclined in such directions, could provide an excellent springboard to a refined and socially progressive conception of the professional interpreter.

1990s Britain seems to prefer deregulation to regulation of working practices. The contemporary view of professionalism, from academics as well as many practitioners, is inclined to the view that there is no helpful distinction to be made between professionals and other expert labourers. Yet, at the same time, where regulation is retained, its use within moral frameworks producing the institutionalisation of responsibility—to oneself and colleagues, to clients, and to the wider polity—can be argued to provide a realistic understanding of professionalism for the 21st century.

BSL/English interpreting, whilst it has been described as an 'emerging profession', under the above characterisation turns out to be rather convincingly established as a contemporary profession, largely due to the successful dissemination and uptake by practitioners of the Codes of Practice/Ethics designed by the regulatory bodies. If we can all keep our nerve and not be damaged by the present trend towards deregulation in the supposed interests of free-marketing, then the BSL/English interpreting profession may yet develop a strong and long-term tenable foundation.

Acknowledgements

Thanks are due to Aaron Brace, Mary Brennan, Richard Brown, Judy Kegl, Marina McIntire, Clive Palmer, Carol Patrie, Kyra Pollitt, Maureen Reed, Sandy Resnick, Ruth Roberts, Granville Tate and Caroline Taylor for comments made in the preparation of this paper. They nevertheless bear no responsibility for the final text.

References

Crompton, R. (1990) Professions in the current context. *Work, Employment & Society* Special Issue, 147–167.

Fenton, S. (1993) Interpreting in New Zealand: An emerging profession. *Journal of Interpretation*, 6/1, 155–165.

Hoyle, E. (1980) Professionalization and deprofessionalization in education. Hyle & Megarry (eds.) *Professional Development of Teachers*. New York, NY.

Katschinka, L. (1988) Interpreting-the future. Picken (ed.) *ITI Conference 2: Translators and Interpreters mean business*.Institute of Translation and Interpreting, London.

Lashmar, P. (1994) Licence to kill. *New Statesman & Society*. 6 May 1994, 16–19.

Manasse, H. (1993) *Code of Practice*: Sign language interpreters' experience. Bristol; University of Bristol unpublished MS.

Merton, R. (1982) Institutionalized altruism: The case of the professions. *Social Research and the Practicing Professions*. Cambridge, MA; Abt Books.

Pollitt, K. (1991) Rational responses. *Signpost*, 4/2:24.

Scott Gibson, L. (1991) Sign language interpreting: An emerging profession. Gregory & Hartley (eds.) *Constructing Deafness*. London/Milton Keynes: Pinter Publishers in association with the Open University.

Turner, G. H. (1991) Random rantings. *Signpost*, 4/1:19.

Agencies, interpreters and the Deaf community: working in harmony?
Frank J. Harrington

Introduction

Over the last few years in this country, there has been a dramatic increase in the number of Sign Language Interpreting Services being offered both by national organisations and small independent units. Some of these offer a complete service, using their own employed interpreters, while others act simply as booking agents, contracting freelance interpreters to work with those who request a service. It is interesting that, because of the way the interpreting profession and interpreting services have developed, no two agencies have been set up in exactly the same way, with the result that their funding agreements and service agreements are different in each case. Some agencies are funded by local authorities, on a corporate basis; others have a number of smaller contracts with particular agencies, such as the social services department. Some have contracts to provide certain services nationwide, while others only provide limited services within a specific geographical area.

The tasks which an agency should need to carry out in order to contract an interpreter are broadly similar in most cases; having received a request to provide a service, they need to find an interpreter that is free at the right time, send them a contract or assignment details, agree a fee if the interpreter is self employed, contact the person requiring the service and confirm the appointment with all concerned. This part of the service provided is generally dealt with in a professional and competent manner, and is an important aspect of the agencies' *raison d'être*. What makes them so attractive to so many service users is the fact that they are a 'one stop shop'. In the past people may have spent hours on the telephone trying to secure the services of a single interpreter. The advent of the agency has meant that they now need only make one call and the agency will do the rest. Most people see the agency's administration fee as a small price to pay for such a trouble free service. This booking and administrative aspect of the service seems to function well, but the quality of interpreting which Deaf people receive once a request has been made can be quite diverse, both amongst agencies which act only as booking agents and those services which employ their own interpreters.

Employed interpreters

There are two main sources of interpreting provision; interpreters who are employed by particular agencies, and self-employed interpreters who provide a freelance service. But whether they use their own employees, or the services of freelance interpreters, the quality of provision on the part of any agency is dependent upon two things; the skills of the interpreters they use, and the financial constraints they may or may not find themselves under.

In 1992/93 there was a tightening of regulations by CACDP with the introduction of Registered Trainee status for those holding a Stage III certificate who were undergoing interpreter training. The purpose of this was to try to ensure that Deaf people receive a consistent basic level of skill from their interpreters. The introduction of NVQ qualifications and the mapping of interpreter training provision which have preceded the introduction of CACDP's new Registration Policy (due to be implemented in 2002) has emphasised further the need for interpreters to be appropriately skilled and qualified. In spite of this, however, it is still possible to find job adverts for interpreter posts asking for people with lower levels of sign communication skill than the recommended minimum, and this practice is found not only in new services, which might be forgiven for lack of knowledge, but also in services which are well established.

Again, from jobs that have been advertised over the past few years, it appears that some agencies are expecting to attract registered trainee and registered qualified interpreters, but are offering salaries which do not reflect their skills or experience. Such posts are often re-advertised due to lack of interest, and may eventually be filled by someone who is not of the standard originally required. If agencies are expecting to attract high quality interpreters, then the issue of fee structures needs to be addressed.

In light of this, what might interpreting agencies be expected to provide for their employees?

1. An Equal Opportunities Policy for employees, which could allow for unbiased recruitment procedures, and fair treatment for both part time and full time staff.
2. An Employees' Grievance Procedure, to allow individual interpreters to comment on inappropriate assignments, and working conditions, and to ensure that they can feel safe in their working environment.
3. Supportive Training Opportunities, to ensure an ongoing quality of provision. Training should not simply the cheapest or quickest training option. It should be chosen, both by the employer and the employee, to best suit the individual's skills and abilities.
4. A willingness to see employees treated no worse, in terms of salary and conditions, than others doing similar jobs for similar organisations.

One would hope that agencies employing interpreters might already have such policies, but it would not be a surprise to find that some employers do not have all or any of these.

Freelance interpreters

Many agencies currently use the services of freelance interpreters, as well as their own staff, to meet the needs of their clients, but there is still a wide variety in the quality of provision. Different agencies see different skill levels held by freelance interpreters, any thing from qualified status to Stage II, as acceptable or appropriate for them to be offered work. There are also be differences in the fee structures which individual agencies have set for themselves and which they are prepared to pay to freelance interpreters. These are primarily issues for the agencies to address in terms both of the quality of service they offer to the consumer, and of their commitment to equal opportunity issues. But these issues also effect freelance interpreters, since they have employment and developmental needs which are broadly similar to those of employed interpreters. The question is whether or not they might expect agencies to support them in meeting these needs, and furthermore, whether the agencies see themselves as being in any way responsible for the continuing development of the profession.

The sort of issues which freelance interpreters might expect the agencies to address are as follows:

1 Equality of opportunity in being offered work appropriate to the individual's skill level.
2 Development of a grievance procedure by which the freelance interpreter might voice their concerns either about assignments or working conditions when working for particular agencies.
3 Agencies should have a responsibility to be involved in providing training opportunities for freelance interpreters. There is a need for some form of agreement or contract between agency and interpreters to allow them to receive training support.

In the interests of increasing the available workforce, and therefore the availability of interpreters to the Deaf community, agencies should have a commitment to provide these, or at least to help freelance interpreters in achieving them for themselves. If agencies were able to show a commitment to achieving some or all of these, we would perhaps see a greater co-operation between freelance interpreters and agencies. While this might be something to work towards for the future, most agencies do not have any current policies regarding support for freelance interpreters. On the contrary, an increasing number of agencies are displaying a preference for employing their own interpreters, for reasons which, while they might make a lot of economic sense, are in danger of compromising the agencies' integrity and the interpreting profession as a whole.

Most agencies depend to a large extent on organisations with statutory responsibilities, such as Health or Social Services, to provide the funding for interpreting services (CACDP 1993, Panel of Four 1992). The majority of funding agreements are based on a financial projection, and for this to work, there needs to be a unit cost for an hourly or daily service. In such cases it is easier and more economical for agencies to provide a service using salaried staff, receiving payment in the form of a grant annually or quarterly, than it is for them to contract and pay different freelance interpreters at different fees for different jobs. Similarly, it is often more economical for a Local Authority to put up a salary and some overheads for an interpreter post, in return for a free service, than to 'spot purchase' a freelance interpreter for every situation.

One of the negative aspects of this philosophy is that Deaf people might be limited in their choice of interpreter. What happens to a Deaf man at a personal hospital appointment if the agency in his area only employs female interpreters? What happens to a Deaf person if they want a skilled, qualified interpreter, but their local agency only has stage II holders on its staff? And how many of these agencies will employ a freelance interpreter specifically requested by a Deaf person, yet leave their own employees in the office with no assignments?

There has been one recent development which is challenging even further the freelance interpreter's right to work freely and without prejudice. A number of agencies now charge freelance interpreters an administration fee for offering them work, and will only offer work to those who have made an agreement with them to pay the fee. While this is not bad business practice, and is in some ways a logical way for the agency to ensure its income, there are a number of potential difficulties which may arise from this practice.

Firstly, any interpreter, regardless of their qualifications, who does not agree to be charged an administration fee will not be contacted for work by the agency. These interpreters might be Qualified or Trainees, and may advertise their availability through publications such as the CACDP Directory, which publishes recommended fees and minimum payments which they are entitled to charge (CACDP Directory 1996). But if the agency advertises itself as the main point of contact for interpreting services in a particular area, these interpreters are effectively being denied the opportunity to work, and the agency is potentially monopolising the market.

Far more serious, however, are the implications for the customer. If the agency has Stage II and Stage III holders on its books, in lieu of the qualified and trainee interpreters who are unwilling to accept their charging policies, then it is possible that someone requiring the services of a qualified interpreter might be denied that service, not because there is no-one available, but simply because the agency is more concerned with its profit margins than with providing a good, high quality service in the best interests of Deaf people.

Some people who work for agencies believe that in future we will see all interpreters employed by agencies, being paid fixed wages, with the agency charging fixed national rates. This again would make life very difficult for freelance interpreters, and could have a number of outcomes. On the one hand, if the freelance market becomes stifled, and interpreters are forced to accept all of their work through the agencies, then there would be no room for people to specialise within the profession, while at the same time, the agencies would have a monopoly of the marketplace.

If on the other hand the agencies dealt with only the community based every day assignments, using only their own employees, and avoided the specialised work, for which there might not be grant funding or the possibility of a contract, then there might be a split in the profession, with the most highly skilled interpreters concentrating on high profile assignments, leaving the everyday needs of the Deaf community to be dealt with by unqualified or inexperienced people.

Neither of these scenarios would be particularly beneficial to Deaf people, the agencies or the interpreting profession, and it is most important that those who provide services do not lose sight of the principal reason for their existence; to meet the needs of the Deaf community.

The influence of Deaf people

This leads on to another issue; the question of how the Deaf community is involved in decisions made about interpreting services. Some of the larger organisations in this country have always tried to consult with service users when establishing services, and this can be seen through Deaf user panels which have been set up in a number of areas. But what impact do such panels have? While they might provide a forum for interested parties to meet occasionally, it is not always the case that in attending such a meeting, these Deaf people have any real influence on the day to day running of their service.

The smaller independent agencies seem to have a greater input from their local Deaf community; a number of organisations have committees which are made up of 50% Deaf people, representing the local Deaf community, and 50% hearing people, who represent the funding bodies. These people have a more direct influence on the way services are run, with the result that no decision which might significantly affect the organisation can be taken without the knowledge and agreement of the Deaf community representatives.

The other main provider of services is the local authority, either social services or health authority. These organisations have statutory responsibilities for service provision, and since the advent of community care legislation, and more recently the Disability Discrimination Act (DDA), the services they offer should be needs led, in consultation with the user. In practice, however, provision is often still dependent upon budgetary constraints rather than being organised according to the wishes, or legal rights, of the client.

Financial implications for the Deaf community

Finally, what part should, or might, Deaf people be expected to play in the funding of interpreting services? In other countries, there is legislation which governs the rights of Deaf people to equality, through the provision of interpreters, for example the Swedish constitution (SDR 1991) and the Americans with Disabilities Act in the USA. The result of such legislation is that there seems to be an unwritten law that a Deaf person should not be charged for an interpreting service. There are of course exceptions, e.g. weddings and other private functions. One specific example from the USA is that of a person selling bulk order products to members of the public, a situation which is considered to be for personal gain, and for which the Deaf person is seen to be responsible for their own communication needs.

Interpreting services in this country have operated a 'no charge' policy for a long time, but is this something which might change in the future? Since October 1994, following the commissioner's decision in the case of Rebecca Halliday, it has been possible for Deaf people to apply for Disability Living Allowance (DLA) on the grounds of their social communication needs. This is something that the Government had been fighting, but their case to have the commissioner's decision overturned in court in May 1995 was not successful (HMSO 1995).

The Government lodged a further appeal to the House of Lords for the ruling to be overturned, but in July 1997 this appeal also failed, with the result that thousands of Deaf people across the country are eligible to claim DLA. DLA is divided into two parts, with an allowance for personal care, and a separate allowance for mobility. Deaf people are eligible to claim up to the middle rate of the care component, and the lower rate of mobility allowance. These claims are allowed on the grounds that Deaf people need to be accompanied on a daily basis by a hearing person to interpret for them in a wide number of situations (House of Lords 1997).

DLA, once granted, is an allowance to be used at the recipient's discretion, and many Deaf people use it to pay for other things more important to them than interpreting services. In fact, those who choose to use the money to pay for their communication support, find that the amount which is awarded to any individual is woefully inadequate to meet the cost of the constant levels of interpreting for which it is intended.

The low rate of the care component is currently £14.20 per week, which amounts to £738.40 p/a, but those who are awarded the middle rate care component and the lower rate mobility component receive £50.00 p/w, which amounts to £2,600 p/a.

Perhaps we should put this into perspective. If a geographical area, such as a county, were to have a population of 800,000 people, then recent figures published by the British Deaf Association (BDA) and Royal National Institute for Deaf People (RNID), and the Office of National Statistics (Davies 1995, HMSO 1995) would suggest that approximately 900 people in that county would be profoundly Deaf British Sign Language (BSL) users. Let us assume that the county has an interpreting agency which employs two interpreters, and also uses the services of local freelance interpreters, operating on an annual budget of £85,000 funded by service level agreements with Local and Health Authorities. If just 33 of the 900 BSL users in the area were receiving the higher amount of DLA, then, added together, the sum would exceed the interpreting agency's total annual budget.

The best possible scenario to come from this is that there could in fact be extra money available for interpreting services, but it is equally possible that the outcome might be less positive. We should not deny Deaf people money to which they are entitled, but on a national level, millions of pounds could be paid out to Deaf people, on the understanding that it will be used to pay for their communication support needs. If the Government is already funding interpreting services through local authorities, they may not want to pay twice for the same service, and in this climate of providing people with the power to purchase the services they need for themselves, it is more likely that the corporate funding would be cut, rather than the money which is being given to individual Deaf people. If corporate funding were to disappear, then the future of regional interpreting services, and interpreters in general would be in the hands and pockets of the Deaf community (see Turner 1995).

Although there is legislation in USA, with the Americans With Disabilities Act, Deaf people do not actually receive any money to pay for interpreting services, or as a specific result of their Deafness. In Norway interpreting services have been provided through a voucher system, but again Deaf people do not actually receive payment as a result of their communication needs. Here in Britain, we have the DDA which is putting the responsibility for provision of access onto service providers (National Disability Council 1994, DDA 1995). This, along with the availability of DLA, could mean that the government might further distance itself from any direct involvement in the provision of interpreting services. This would leave Deaf people to finance their own communication support from their DLA payments on occasions when there is not an employer or service provider who will accept this responsibility. Whether or not this will, or should, happen is open to debate, but it is one of the logical conclusions to which these recent developments might lead.

Conclusion

Sign language interpreting is still a relatively new phenomenon, and in this country, many of the interpreting agencies are less than five years old, and it is only natural that there are differences in the way services are provided, and difficulties in actually providing them. But the issue is far greater than simply the survival of the agency. Deaf people have needs which are served by interpreters and interpreting agencies, among other services, and it is most important that they should be actively involved in decisions which are made about the provision of such services. Interpreters, both employed and freelance have concerns relating to their employment and continued professional development, and the agencies and those who fund them have responsibilities relating to the quality of services they provide.

If Deaf people, agencies, interpreters, and those who pay for the services can work together with mutual respect and understanding, then interpreting services will improve and thrive, but this can only be achieved with the mutual trust and co-operation of all involved.

References and bibliography

CACDP (1993) *Agents for Change*. CACDP: Durham.

—— (1996) *Directory*. CACDP: Durham. 1:1,1–23.

Davies, A. (1995) *Hearing In Adults*. Whurr: England.

Department of Social Security. (1995) Ruling of the Court of Appeal in the case of the Secretary of State v Fairey. Transcript of the Ruling.

HMSO (1995) *Disability Discrimination Act 1995*: Chapter 50. HMSO: London.

—— (1995) *Health and Social Services Statistics*. HMSO: London.

House of Lords (1997) *Judgment—Secretary of State for Health v. Fairey*. HMSO: London.

National Disability Council (1994): Disability—On the Agenda. Disability Discrimination Bill, (Consultation Papers).

Panel of Four (1992) *Communication is Your Responsibility: the Commission of Enquiry into Human Aids to Communication*. John Knight: England.

Padden, C. (1980) The Deaf Community and the Culture of Deaf People. In C. Baker and R. Battison (eds) *Sign Language and the Deaf Community:*

Essays in honour of William C. Stokoe. National Association of the Deaf: Silver Spring MD. 89–104.

Swedish National Association of the Deaf (1991) *Action Program on Interpreting Services*. SDR, Leksand: Sweden.

Turner, G.H. (1995) Rights and Responsibilities: The Relationship between Deaf people and Interpreters. *Deafness* 11/3.

Woodward, J. (1972) Implications for Sociolinguistic Research among the Deaf. *Sign Language Studies*, 1:1–7.

The code and the culture: sign language interpreting —in search of the new breed's ethics
Granville Tate and Graham H. Turner

Introduction

Analyses of the role and responsibilities of sign language interpreters have continued to develop since the 'emergence' of the profession (Scott Gibson 1991). The nature of the relationship between service providers and consumers has been of concern in the field (Turner 1995 and 1996). In the UK and elsewhere, Codes of Ethics/Practice have been a principal tool used to guide professional behaviour, and they have been revised to take into account changing experiences in interpreting praxis as well as changing theoretical underpinnings.

What no Code can do is to anticipate all possible situations in which an interpreter may find her/himself and offer an 'off-the-peg' solution to whatever dilemmas may arise. So interpreters make sense of problems, and find 'spur-of-the-moment' strategies to address them, based upon their best understanding of the spirit of the Code, adherence to which is a condition of their registration status. Just as the rules of any sport evolved over time as players and umpires faced newly challenging situations on the field of play, so interpreters in these early years of professionalism have been required to 'play the game' in the best way they can.

The question asked in this paper focuses upon one particular aspect of the role of an interpreter, seeking to explore the perspective upon it highlighted in the profession's ethical guidelines and practitioners' interpretations of those guidelines in situated communication events. Our starting point was a sense that in some ethically complex contexts, either the strictures of the Code itself or interpreters' readings of its prescriptions were often at odds with actual practice. The aim, then, was to begin to look a little more carefully, from the interpreter's point of view, at some problem circumstances and thus to get a handle on some apparent discrepancies between the profession's encoded regulatory principles and their practical realisation.

In the following pages, therefore, we firstly set out briefly some of the underpinning knowledge informing our own approach to the issue; secondly, sketch the context in which our study was undertaken; thirdly, present the 'dilemma' scenarios highlighted and exemplify interpreters' responses to them, offering our perspective on the messages embedded in these responses; and finally, suggest a number of pointers to future developments.

Codes and models

Interpreting practice in England, Wales and Northern Ireland is subject to regulation by the Council for the Advancement of Communication with Deaf People (CACDP). This body publishes and promulgates the *Code of Ethics* to which BSL/English interpreters are professionally bound to adhere. The Code is not explicitly wedded to any particular model of interpreters and interpreting, but the *zeitgeist* in the field inevitably leads to the materialisation at any particular time of a 'professional culture' tending towards certain norms. In the UK's case, we would argue—having been involved in providing, co-ordinating and using interpreting services, as well as in the training of interpreters—that the dominant model of interpreting has been of the 'machine' kind (the interpreter is seen as essentially just a device that takes no part in communicative proceedings other than dispassionately to relay messages between individuals not sharing a common language—cf Roy 1993). Bound up inextricably with this, we believe, the CACDP Code is often *taken both to prescribe and to reflect* this kind of 'machine' model.

Broadly-speaking, machine interpreting has been seen—in all relevant sectors of the community—as a tool of empowerment for Deaf people. Simply put, machines do what they're told. They're under instruction: no instruction, no action. Machines don't generate their own contributions to the job in hand: they simply respond as programmed to external stimuli (levers pulled, buttons pressed, etc). In part, early versions of interpreting Codes erred on the side of caution with respect to seeking to ensure that the stipulated role of the interpreter was essentially reactive and not proactive. To a certain extent, this was doubtless a response to the view that, prior to the emergence of interpreting as defined occupation, Deaf people had too often been preceded through life's doors by hearing people saying "What he/she wants is..." The Code made clear that the aim was for the interpreter to open the door, but first across the threshhold, setting and executing their own agenda, would be the Deaf consumer.

This sense that interpreters have a significant but limited part to play in providing access to communication and information for Deaf people continues to be very real and to help define current role-norms. People fear less machine-like models because they risk dis-empowering Deaf people—anything other than machine can be hard to distinguish from a paternalistic 'follow me through the door' approach. However, the ideologically normative strength of the perspective which says that it is only proper for the interpreter to be entirely uninvolved and mechanised—facilitated by its tidy 'black-and-whiteness', the unambiguous directives for action which it conveniently supplies—has created a situation where, we would argue, professionals in the field have been reluctant openly to look at what they know actually happens in many situations. This is made difficult since strictures concerning confidentiality within the Code make it hard (if not impossible) to find a professionally proper space in which interpreters are able to discuss the resolution of role-dynamic dilemmas. The hegemony of 'machine is the only way because it's the only way to be uninvolved' has created a conspiracy of silence—not an actively desired one on the part of practitioners, but one which they feel duty-bound to observe nonetheless—about the very real disempowering effects of a blanket aspiration to machine-like behaviour. It has created a reluctance to talk about how interpreters are involved in interpreting situations and how they do generate action, make choices and exercise decisive power in hidden and not-so-hidden ways. This very conspiracy forces interpreters into the position of making their discretionary choices and exercising power covertly with the result that individual interpreters find themselves resolving in isolation the inevitable role conflicts of their job (Cooke 1995).

Perhaps the barrier to open discussion of this issue has its roots in the early development of interpreting as a distinct occupational role. At the time, there was a need, on the one hand, to carve out a distinct area of expertise and, on the other, to be seen to be operating from a perspective different from that of social/welfare work, which was often seen as patronising and controlling. The professional position is, in the UK, now being carved out fairly clearly. Interpreting is now a maturing occupation. It has broken away from social work. The pressure toward a 'machine' perspective which existed in the early days—and perhaps was a necessary stage to go through—has diminished. This allows us to seek to explore definitions of roles and responsibilities in other ways.

Engaging with reality

At this point we would like to take up a number of hypothetical dilemmas. We can think of them as becoming dilemmas partly because the Code is—in itself—too stark to tell interpreters how to negotiate the many varied and complex real-life situations which they encounter. Training and apprenticeship should flesh out this ethical skeleton and give it a practical dimension—but part of the 'conspiracy' to date has been the unaddressed impoverishment of processes and procedures that would give substance to any such assurance. The Code by itself, and the mechanistic role model it has most commonly been taken to endorse, lack the textured richness or are too one-dimensional always to enable interpreters to act in ways suitable for the situation. In fact, this Code-role can sometimes seem to disable interpreters by encouraging them to act in one way when they know they could be more effective if they acted in another way which seems to them to contradict the Code.

The hypothetical dilemmas that follow were put to interpreters[1] for their anonymous responses. These are dilemmas which may occur at any time in an interpreter's career. We tried to draw upon situations from our own experiences and from those passed on to us by other interpreters. We asked respondents to try to answer in terms of what they felt they really would do—rather than what they felt they were supposed to do—if they found themselves in these situations. As an attempt to begin to grapple with actual professional behaviour, this is, we recognise, in itself methodologically inadequate: however, all studies have their limitations—if these are acknowledged for what they are, the results may still be of value. What is most significant in this case, we would suggest, is respondents' articulation of why they have given a particular set of answers.

Given that the approach to questioning adopted here was open-ended (we didn't use a multiple-choice or otherwise readily quantifiable procedure), the statistics we have generated—in each case, we give a figure for those taking relatively mechanistic vs non-mechanistic stances—are based upon *our* interpretative perceptions as analysts of the implications of the response data. Again, we make no attempt to hide any methodological weaknesses. We originally posed six of these hypothetical questions, but have selected four for this paper. These four all revolve, in our view, around some aspect of the role-model issue: specifically, all four pertain to the mechanistic nature, or otherwise, of interpreter behaviour, the use of professional judgement, and interpreter-generated input to the interactional event.

The scenarios and analysis of responses
1. *Tablets scenario*

—You are interpreting with a Deaf patient visiting her GP. She is prescribed a drug called Visapan (which the doctor says is powerful) to be taken once a day. In your interpretation you fingerspell the name. The Deaf person nods calmly and signs "Is it okay to take several vitamins at once?" You interpret the question to the doctor and she says "Yes, of course, that's no problem". You are aware that there has been a misunderstanding, i.e. that the Deaf person is referring to the Visapan as vitamins. You have interpreted everything by the book. What do you do, and why?

In this situation some 99% prefer non-mechanistic options. Only one respondent indicated that they would not generate any input of their own. Two examples which we took to be indicative of non-mechanistic responses:

1a "Forget the book and enable communication."
1b "I have to live with myself not the *Code of Practice*."

2. *Baby scenario*

—You are interpreting with a Deaf mother-to-be when she goes for a scan. You know that she doesn't want to know the sex of her baby, but the gynaecologist suddenly comes out with the information that it's a boy! What do you do, and why?

Of the respondents to this question, approximately 77% stated that they would make some kind non-mechanistic intervention, while some 23% felt that they would not. Here are two examples of responses from the first group. The first example is representative of the vast majority of responses:

2a "I think I would tell her that the doctor has just said the sex but 'you don't want to know, right?' (also explain what I said to the doctor). It's difficult 'cos if hearing the slip would have been heard."

2b "Don't tell the mum, but explain to the doctor that you are not going to tell her."

Now two examples of replies from the second group:

2c "Interpret the info, i.e., do the job."

2d "I would sign 'it's a boy' because (i) the mother should have made it clear that she did not want to know or (ii) if she had made that clear and the doctor forgot then a hearing person would have heard and by my signing it the deaf woman would be equal to a hearing woman."

Discussion 1 and 2

A key part of the Code at present is its prescription that nothing should be added to or omitted from the meaning of what is uttered by the principal interacting parties. In both of these scenarios a very high percentage of respondents say they would use a non-mechanistic strategy of some kind. How many real-life situations occur, we find ourselves wondering, where this part of the Code is pragmatically sidestepped? It might be argued that the Code as it stands may not be helping or enabling interpreters to function optimally in such situations. It can create anxiety because it is seen as inappropriate in some situations.

Certain questions, we feel, arise from this which demand to be aired. Why do the overwhelming majority of interpreters, many of whom will be qualified and with experience, feel that in these circumstances adherence to the Code guidelines would need to be suspended? Are they misunderstanding the intention of the Code? If so, why are they doing so? Does their feeling actually accord more closely with Deaf consumers' wishes than the alternative would do? And if the Code is not achieving its aim, what is to be done?

With the *Tablets* scenario the reasoning behind the view that adherence to the Code is secondary is easily understood: the gravity of the situation.

1c "When you are dealing in any area with crucial results such as this I think the interpreter has a responsibility to ensure all info is clearly understood."

1d "This could be a serious error that I am not prepared to live with."

What is very clear from many of the responses is that practitioners feel that the Code specifies a particular role from which they must sometimes depart in order to work effectively. From these responses it would appear that interpreters feel their actual practice may not always conform to the Code-model which guides them. As one respondent comments:

1e "Step out of role—sign and speak: 'I believe there has been a misunderstanding—are Visapan vitamins?' Step back into role. This can easily happen. I am responsible for communication."

This respondent is appealing to another set of guidelines to inform practice. The interpreter's own 'common sense' alternatives have come to the rescue here—developed through knowledge and experience of interpreting and working with the Deaf community. 'I am responsible for communication' is almost a definition of an alternative non-mechanistic model (cf the 'dialogue director' model as described in Tate, 1996). But something seems to us to be going wrong if interpreters genuinely feel that to take the above course of action forces them to act in a way that is actually contrary to their professional Code: either the Code needs to say something different, or the way that interpreters are enculturated into their professional understanding of that Code needs to change. Either way, we would argue that there is much to be learned from seeking to be aware of and work with the best of practitioners' learned experiences.

Those interpreters who chose not to 'intervene' appear to see the same boundaries to good practice as prescribed by the Code's account of their role; the key difference is that they present themselves as preferring not to overstep those boundaries, even in these circumstances. Characteristic of these respondents was the person who, citing the exact sections of the Code which he/she felt disbarred him/her from doing anything other than this, said:

2e "Nothing, because to do something means that I have to step out of my role as an interpreter."

3. Interview scenario

—You are interpreting for a Deaf person at a job interview. There are no other candidates. While interpreting, you realise that the way the Deaf person is presenting himself in BSL is not going to ensure a positive outcome for him. You know for sure that this Deaf person can do the job superbly. You could polish your voice-over to be in line with the interviewer's expectations... What do you do, and why?

In this case, some 68% of respondents claimed that they would straightforwardly reflect the Deaf person's signing without any kind of 'intervention'. Meanwhile, 32% suggested that they would, in the event, look for one or another non-mechanistic strategy, even if doing so left them feeling rather uncomfortable.

Discussion

To us as we set the question, this scenario opened up the possibility of learning something about the extent to which interpreters felt they should, in fact, be 'part-advocate' by leaning towards support for Deaf people's interests where possible and appropriate. This is clearly one of the most significant areas for attention in the current search for a rapprochement between mechanistic and non-mechanistic approaches to interpreting (see Scott Gibson 1995). In addition, there was scope for discovery in relation to practitioners' views of the limits of cultural mediation.

Many respondents in fact answered as if the question were a test of their impartiality, as two examples make clear:

3a "Not my responsibility to ensure candidate presents well."
3b "If I polish up the voice-over too much the interviewer may be present at a future occasion when the Deaf person is interpreted by another interpreter... They will smell a fish."

The general theme of the responses in this category was, as more than one person stated:

3c "Give the best voice-over you can to reflect the Deaf person ... "

However, this offers no explanation of what it would mean to 'reflect' the Deaf person in their voice-over. One of the respondents also offers:
3d "But take into account cultural differences—to be fair."

The issue of what constitutes cultural mediation is one that emerges awash with question marks here. Does the Code enshrine the kind of 'polishing' referred to here as 'permissible' behaviour, or not? When does smoothing over cultural gaps become an exercise in sheer creativity as opposed to one evolving naturally from the resources of a given situation?

Sixteen people explicitly (and a few more by implication) permitted themselves—using phrases such as "higher level English but without any additions"—to make adjustments to register, although a number equally explicitly stated that they absolutely would not countenance what were perceived as content improvements. Relatedly, a number of comments carried the implication that the voice-over should be formal almost irrespective of what the Deaf person is doing:
3e "Match English register to interviewer voice."

This seems odd. Of course one goes into a situation expecting to produce language that is appropriate, but judging that appropriacy is a very delicate matter, not at all simply a matter of getting out the 'Interview-speak' file before the session and using it come what may. This suggests that a considerable proportion of interpreters do not appreciate the impact of variation of this order. So the person who wrote:
3f "I would possibly consider raising the register although I would not consider interpreting what has not been said. Nor would I embellish."

patently does not acknowledge that 'raising the register' at one's own discretion is embellishment of sorts and as such is non-mechanistic.

A proportion of this group of non-mechanistic respondents would intervene in ways where the reasoning is not linguistic/cultural. Some of the comments here suggested a strong desire to act in a kind of advoca-tive capacity. These respondents wanted, for instance, to:
3g "Try to encourage the Deaf person to give more personal facts."
3h "Explain to employer the candidate's presentation."

4. Court scenario

—A young Deaf man has been loitering around his old school. He has been warned off many times with increasing severity. The headmaster has finally become fed up and the matter has gone to court. In court, the magistrate sentences the man to be banned from coming within 500 yards of the school. Nobody has pointed out to the court what place a Deaf school has in the cultural life of such a person. The magistrate seems to be a reasonable sort of chap... Do you say anything, and why?

The majority of respondents (69%) feel that they would not say anything, either directly in court or indirectly outwith the formal proceedings to the solicitors or the Deaf man. Many of these people make reference to the view that it is not within their role to take any action here. However, almost one third (31%) say that they would say something to someone.

Discussion

Once again we see in the responses a clear readiness to reply in terms of a delimited role-bound territory within which the interpreter is empowered to act:

4a "No—not my responsibility [...] In any case the Deaf person deserves it. There's not a whisper of a dilemma here."

The non-mechanistic respondents here can be divided into direct and indirect 'interveners'. The latter would offer information but would seek, so far as the court is concerned, to do so in a discreet and diplomatic way, outwith formal proceedings:

4b. "Yes, I feel it is part of my role to bridge cultural gaps [...] I would probably ask to speak to the defence lawyer in the presence of the Deaf man."

Others would seek to speak directly to the court:

4c "I would ask if it was possible to say something on his behalf."

4d "I would refer the magistrate to... [Deaf organisations]."

The overriding question for an interpreter in this situation is, 'is there justification for saying something to someone?' If it is agreed that the court system may be discriminating against the Deaf man by not being aware of the place the school has in the cultural life of such a person, then the interpreter may be the only one to see how this may affect the outcome. Therefore, the question needing to be asked is, is it ethically proper not to say anything? This is different to assuming that the Deaf man is either guilty as charged or not. Some respondents clearly do take a view about whether the man is guilty and use this as a reason for not saying anything:

4e "No way. He broke the law and it's up to justice to deal with him. I am not an advocate."

Of course, this example is one in which the factors affecting any decision interact in complex ways. We do not wish to draw any over-simplistic conclusions from it. What does come across, however, is that there is an ethical dimension to interpreters' decision-making in such a context which is neither accounted for nor entirely guided by the predicted Code-model. Whatever their reasoning—in terms of legality, morality, professionalism and so forth—almost one third of respondents to the survey feel that they would take a non-mechanistic line.

Summary of statistics

scenario	non-mechanistic	mechanistic
Tablet	99%	1%
Baby	77%	23%
Interview	68%	32%
Court	31%	69%

Conclusions

The summary above fundamentally shows that the dominant, mechanistic Code-model does not accord fully with interpreters' own views on their own professional practices: if it did, the left-hand column would (at the very least) consistently feature much smaller numbers than the right. Our key early response to the comments returned by practising interpreters to these questions was that there needed to be a fuller reworking of the Code which would guide interpreters more explicitly on how to respond in the face of dilemmas such as these. This view has shifted over time, so that we would now argue that it is not so much the Code which should change—though complacency is never healthy—so much as the professional culture which it is designed to reflect and engender. Pivotal to such change are (a) the educational processes by which practitioners are enculturated and (b) the articulation of the ethical values which underpin the wording of the published Code.

Facing up to any residual complacency, it is possible that the Code can still valuably be revised so that it guides interpreters into ethically engaged choices—such as they already make—instead of saying 'it's not my responsibility to have an ethical view'. They would thus be enabled to make their choices feeling humane, empowered and professional instead of humane but disempowered and professionally negligent.

Nevertheless, the survey responses suggest to us that interpreters would welcome the availability of guidance on good practice when faced with such dilemmas. The establishment of a resource base which pooled information on strategies adopted in real situations—in other words, where experienced professionals' own interpretations of their Code guidelines were respected and could be accessed to inform future practice—might in itself be a positive step which would clearly acknowledge the inadequacy of any assumption that professional behaviour is unproblematic.

We would argue for the value of using interpreters' experiences in dealing with tricky situations to develop more comprehensive guidelines enabling practitioners to negotiate the complexities and unexpectedness of many real-life situations. When dilemmas occur, and people find good, solid, satisfactory solutions or strategies for dealing with them, then there ought to be an ongoing attempt to codify those strategies in some kind of annex to the basic Code (which represents core interpreter values or ethics). An ever-evolving form of the Code can then develop a kind of 'case law'. It would not provide all the answers but it would offer interpreters knowledge of how seemingly anomalous or ambiguous situations may be negotiated skilfully whilst still keeping in touch with those basic ethics.

Regulatory bodies for interpreting may declare that they want and encourage and even expect interpreters to use the Code 'sensibly', by taking it as a guideline and letting 'common sense' decide. The problem is that 'common sense' is not common to all. Therefore our conclusion—supported, we would argue, by the variability in responses to our survey questions, and the comments made by interpreters in answering those questions—is that interpreters are looking for more fully articulated written guidelines and a more fully developed education in how to use the Code with sensitivity to context.

At present, our experience is that we face a situation where many interpreters actually expect the Code to guide them in some simple black-and-white fashion: they want the Code to tell them exactly what to do. If our perception is accurate (and we feel that this survey helps to confirm that it is), then it needs to be better established during the education of interpreters that grey goes with the territory, and that would-be professionals had better learn to live with it, and indeed to embrace it. Being able to act competently within the grey zone is an integral part of their professionalism. Enabling trainees to get to grips with this—including learning the underpinning values and reaching an understanding of the complexity and multi-dimensionality of their practical application—will take time and probably substantial periods of apprenticeship.

In conclusion, we would wish to reiterate the need for resistance of the conspiracy of silence. Within interpreting agencies and through interpreting associations, in particular, ways must be found to facilitate the proper exploration of professional dilemmas. (To take one instance, this study threw a harsh light upon the extent to which the notion of 'cultural mediation' may presently be papering over cracks.) This can be done with consumers and fellow practitioners to the benefit of all parties.

Finally, once again (cf Turner 1996), we feel that the study gives evidence for the view that interpreters are typically very ready to relate their actions to the Code—for better or worse. This in itself, we stress, is evidence of a real willingness to accept a fully regulated professional approach which in itself, in principle, gives a very solid foundation.

Notes

1 There were a total of 103 replies to the questionnaire: 51 Registered Trainee interpreters and 48 Registered Qualified interpreters. There were 33 male and 70 female respondents. The study began as part of a larger questionnaire survey composed by a group of postgraduate students and supervised primarily by Mary Brennan, along with

contributions from David Brien and Richard Brown (as members of the team of the Deaf Studies Research Unit, University of Durham). The group of students involved in the entire survey included Hettie May Bailey, Andrew Cornes, Helena Forsman, Jean Green, Aprile Harman, Sheenagh Hull, Fr. Peter McDonough, Sean Nicholson, George Reynolds, Granville Tate, Rae Than and Graham Turner. The 'Ethics' section of the questionnaire was devised by the authors of this paper along with Helena Forsman. Helena was not able to contribute to the writing of this paper and, along with the others named above, bears no responsibility for its content. We would wish to acknowledge the contribution made to the development of our thinking on these issues by all of the above-named people as well as by module tutors including Judith Collins, Bill Moody, Marie Jean Philip, Kyra Pollitt, Maureen Reed and Liz Scott Gibson.

Bibliography

Cooke, M. (1995) Review of K. Laster and V. Taylor (1994) Interpreters and the Legal System, Sidney, The Federation Press. *Forensic Linguistics* 2/1: 126–132.

Roy C. B. (1993) The Problem with Definitions, Descriptions and the Role Metaphors of Interpreters. *Journal of Interpretation* 6/1: 127–154.

Scott Gibson, L. (1991) Sign Language Interpreting: An Emerging Profession. In Gregory, S. and Hartley, G. M. (eds) *Constructing Deafness*. Open University Press, Milton Keynes. 253–258.

Tate, G. (1996) Elements of a Model of the Community Interpreter: Dialogue Interpreting and a *Code of Practice*. Unpublished MS, DSRU, University of Durham.

Turner, G. H. (1995) Rights and Responsibilities: The Relationship between Deaf people and Interpreters. *Deafness* 11/3: 4–8.

—— (1996) Regulation and responsibility: The Relationship between Interpreters and Deaf people. *Deaf Worlds* 12/1: 1–7.

Interpreting assignments: should I or shouldn't I?
Graham H. Turner

In April 1995, CACDP launched its revamped (and retitled) *Code of Ethics* for interpreters. The revisions were derived from a long and careful consultation process and there'll no doubt be ongoing work to refine and tighten both the Code itself and practitioners' interpretations of it. As an initial small contribution to that process, I'd like to offer some thoughts in relation to assignment complexity.

Item three of the new Code states: "Interpreters shall not accept work which, having taken relevant factors into account, they judge to be beyond their competence." It's important that further thought is given to the notion of relevant factors. Which factors are these? Do they change from one occasion to the next? Is there any way to put the assessment of relevant factors onto a more controlled footing? Many questions present themselves.

We're not talking here about actual qualifications or the level at which a person is registered with CACDP. It's not the case that Registered Qualified interpreters don't find any assignments complex. They do. 'Real 'terps never blink' is neither a realistic nor a desirable attitude to take. But it would take a major change in the occupational culture for RQSLIs to begin to feel more comfortable about saying 'No, that is an assignment I do not feel happy to accept'. Mind you, of course, some people already do this. You can see in the CACDP Directory, for instance, that some people choose to add notes indicating that they don't wish to be offered certain types of work.

For freelance interpreters, of course, saying 'no' may be a great deal easier than it is for those employed by agencies. It may therefore be most pressing for agencies to consider the basis upon which they can sensibly appoint individual interpreters to assignments. Nobody is well served by mismatches. Consumers don't get full access to information. Interpreters are put into situations where they may be left professionally vulnerable—this must surely contribute to 'burn-out' and the disappearance of self-confidence. Employing agencies may lose work

First published in 1995, in *Standard*. CACDP, August 1995.

and goodwill, alienating elements of their client group, if they do not take sufficient care in supplying services. And so forth.

If there is more to judging assignment complexity than 'needs RQSLI' and 'RTSLI adequate', as I'm suggesting, then what dimensions might these judgments also take into account? Here are a round dozen for your consideration. (They are neither in any particular order nor necessarily all equal in weight.)

1 *Preparability*. A lot of what we still tend to call 'interpretation' might really more appropriately seen as 'translation', since it's rehearsed, reworked, edited and polished before the final agreed version is ever put into the public domain. There's a vast gulf between this and, for instance, interpreting an unexpected news flash that suddenly reaches the newsreader's desk halfway through the BBC2 morning transmission. The more preparable an assignment is, other things being equal, the less complex it might be considered.

2 *Directionality*. Although tradition has it that conference interpreting is hard and therefore carries greater status than liaison interpreting, there are surely some aspects of conference work that ease the burden considerably. Primary among these might be the fact that the conference interpreter has to think largely in terms of only 'one-way traffic' at any given time. Conferences are not conversations, for the most part: they're serial monologues. The result is that the interpreter typically doesn't have the strain of trying to 'manage' conveying contributions from two or more different directions at once. In contrast to this, a workshop or open forum in which contributions can come from five, ten, fifty different directions without warning might be seen to be more difficult to handle.

3 *Stoppability*. Since most BSL/English interpreting is done in simultaneous mode, the cognitive load for the interpreter can be tremendous. Nobody's brain can process such material without error or fatigue indefinitely. However, some interpreting assignments might be seen as being more tolerant of interpreter interventions—for whatever reason—than others. I've been to conferences, for instance, where there has been an 'unofficial' interpreter whose attempts to stop the presenter have been very frostily received. On the other hand, if the interpreter is 'official' and recognised as part and parcel of ensuring that the confer-

ence message reaches the audience, then interventions are much more readily accepted. This is one reason, too, why many interpreters report police work to be less stressful than court work, the willingness to check and retrace steps being seen to be that much greater in police station interviews.

4 *Sensitivity*. Since interpreters are—until machine translation improves greatly!—human beings, consideration must be given to the sensitivity of the assignment and the interpreter's experience and ability to handle delicate matters in a calm and composed manner. Bereavement counselling, for instance, might be considered among the more demanding kind of assignments on this basis.

5 *Role multiplicity*. Linked but not equivalent to directionality, this factor refers to the number and range of different role-players participating in any kind of interpreted scenario. In a classroom, for instance, there may be 30 potential speakers/signers, but they'll typically either be teachers or pupils. In a courtroom, in contrast, there may be lay witnesses, expert witnesses, defendants, solicitors, barristers, magistrates/judges, jurors, clerks, ushers, and so forth, each of whom has a specific role to play. The interpreter has to cope with them all.

6 *Language: familiarity*. Although the dialects of BSL have yet to be fully mapped out, it's widely known that there's considerable variation within the language. Some of the variation is regional (e.g. the famously unusual number system of Manchester), some is social (e.g. many Gay men use some markedly different signs), some is dependent upon age, and so on. No interpreter is equally at home with all varieties, and being faced with a kind of signing which is unfamiliar can make an assignment a great deal harder to handle.

7 *Language: plurality*. The larger the consumer group at any one assignment, the more likely it is that there will be variation within that group. One result of this is that the chances of the interpreter being able to please everyone are liable to get smaller. Thus, the more variation in signing preferences within a consumer group, the more difficult the assignment is likely to be in respect of language choices.

8 *Language: technicality*. Well-prepared interpreters know that knowledge of the word-formation patterns of BSL and English will help them to deal with unknown terminology. Still, it remains true that

language which is peppered with technical or rarely-used vocabulary will, in all likelihood, be harder to deal with than more everyday speech/signing. Everyone's mental lexicon runs out at some point and reaching that point will compound feelings of strain.

9 *Adaptability*. Here I have in mind not the adaptability of the interpreter, but that of the consumers. Some consumers are more widely experienced than others, of course. They can make allowances for an interpreter who isn't entirely confident with the material to be processed. They can, as it were, make adjustments and 'tune in' to the wavelength the interpreter is using. An audience composed of such people will make the assignment less daunting for the interpreter. Needless to say, this is no excuse for an interpreter willfully to switch onto autopilot while their audience works overtime to reprocess garbled messages!

The remaining three items should perhaps best be considered together as a subset of the twelve. They each cover issues that, in a better world, would and should not necessarily be relevant. Some readers may feel that they have no place in this context and that reaching towards that better world entails rising above such concerns. Others may feel that it is a matter of straightforward realism and pragmatism to include them. If they are not included explicitly, the argument might go, then you can be sure that people will take them into account 'on the quiet'. So I set them up in full knowledge that they perhaps ought to be knocked down.

10 *Preservability*. Some interpreting assignments will be transient. Others will, for one reason or another, be recorded for posterity. It's human nature that the latter will be seen to put more pressure on the interpreter. This is absolutely not to say that the interpreter should be careless of any errors so long as there's no recorded proof of their work. Being courageous enough to deal with one's own errors is a matter of professionalism, ethics and the ability to sleep at night with an untroubled conscience. Nevertheless, if an interpreter goes into an assignment with legs like jelly because they are aware of the presence of video or television cameras, audiotape recorders or detailed text notetakers (as in court), then they are correspondingly less likely, I suspect, to do the job to the best of their ability. It takes considerable self-assurance to forge

ahead knowing that you may be challenged to defend the evidence of your work. No-one will then be well served. It's in this sense that it might be considered relevant to be realistic.

11 *Scrutiny*. The presence of human observers can be as alarming as that of mechanical ones like videocameras (even if the humans don't have photographic memories!). Not all interpreters cope equally well when faced with an audience including, say, the Chief Executives of national organisations working with Deaf people, or an audience composed of fellow interpreters. Once again, let me stress that the point is not that it is, in any facile sense, all right for less highly regarded interpreters to serve Joe Public whilst only the select few should be booked when the Big Boss is in town. Even highly regarded interpreters can go to pieces under pressure. It is a matter of taking the pragmatic view that an interpreter who is affected by such considerations is less likely to produce the goods in the shape of quality interpretations. Of course, there'll be fine judgements required as to when someone reaches the point where they should begin to undertake such work, and there are strong arguments for allowing this to happen only under supervision.

12 *Perceived difficulty*. The previous two points have both acknowledged that the interpreter is a human actor, and not a robot, whose ability to work effectively may be adversely affected by their own perception that the assignment presents exceptional pressures. The final item completes this subset. There may be all manner of other reasons for an individual interpreter to perceive a certain situation as difficult. For instance, if the interpreter has had bad experiences as a patient, he or she may have developed a genuine fear of hospitals. It would be counter-productive, in such circumstances, to send such an interpreter to undertake major hospital assignments. Again, the service to consumers would suffer, and the human cost to the interpreter could well be considerable. This is not a recipe for saying 'the interpreter should be able to pick and choose assignments at whim'. It merely suggests that, as one among the whole set of twelve factors to consider, it may be as well to take into account the individual's own perceptions regarding assignment complexity.

These, then, are a dozen possible 'relevant factors' for consideration. I haven't prioritised at all within this set. Readers may nevertheless see some of these items as more significant than others. It's important to recognise, I think, that no single element should be considered conclusive in isolation: it seems more sensibly to be a matter of building up a picture taking all of these 'relevant factors' into account wherever appropriate. To give just one example of the result when the bigger picture is addressed, item 11 above would suggest that an assignment involving a Big Boss figure would score highly in terms of difficulty. But the Big Boss may use the interpreter's own dialect of BSL and may be very ready and willing to make any necessary reprocessing adjustments in order to cope with the interpreter's output, and on these counts the score would therefore be relatively low. So it's the cumulative effect of consideration of all of these factors that should be taken into account.

The above schema represents the merest scratching of the surface of what is clearly a matter for much discussion and debate. Individual interpreters and service managers will have their own ideas, and quite probably their own formulas for deciding what assignment requires what skills. I don't doubt that many people will disagree with some or all of these suggestions. I hope this article will be stimulating to readers and that people will put forward their own views and experiences on what's missing, what needs clarification, and perhaps even what's useful—if anything!—in relation to this framework.

2
ANALYSES OF INTERPRETING PRACTICES
Education

Deaf students and the interpreted classroom: the effect of translation on education?

Frank J. Harrington

Abstract

In the past decade we have seen a dramatic increase in the numbers of Deaf students entering higher education institutions. As a result, the higher education sector has found it necessary to focus its attentions on the needs of these students, and in the UK a number of projects have been funded to address these issues. Many of the projects have resulted in the establishment of sign language classes for hearing people, or deaf awareness sessions for university staff. Others have focused on the provision of technical aids, and some have led to the provision of an interpreter or communication support worker posts.

Few, if any, however, have gone beyond the question of provision to look at the effect of these services on the students, or their success in terms of giving access to the curriculum.

The aim of this paper is to look at the various forms of support available to deaf students and their effectiveness in terms of providing access to the message of the classroom. It will explore, in particular, what might happen in a classroom or lecture hall where a Deaf student, using the services of a sign language interpreter, is present. In doing so, it will draw upon personal experiences of classroom interpreting, and upon some findings and observations made by other interpreters and researchers both in the UK, Europe and the USA. It will look at how the need for, and provision of support affects Deaf students in terms of their learning capability, and will look at the way in which the situation might affect lecturers and the other hearing students.

It will offer some conclusions about the effectiveness of the interpreted classroom as a place of learning, and suggest ways in which this situation might be improved for all concerned.

Paper given at *The Accessible Millennium*: Exchanging Resources and Tools for a Barrier-free Future, Third International Conference on higher education and Disability. Innsbruck, Austria, 15 July 1998.

Introduction

The communication needs of D/deaf students in higher education are wide and diverse, and are dependent upon a number of factors. It is not enough merely to assume that deafness is uniform, or that all D/deaf people have the same experiences or needs. Rather, it is important to recognise that the experience of deafness is unique to each individual student. The way in which students are able to function, or indeed choose to function in the classroom, will be dependent upon a range of factors and choices based on their own experiences as D/deaf people. Relevant factors might include: their degree of their deafness; their previous educational experience; the level to which they are dependent upon mechanical aids, if at all, and their chosen mode of communication (Webster and Ellwood 1986, Cokely 1990, Winston 1994, Barnes 1996).

As a result, the support they will choose to use in order to access the message of the classroom will be similarly varied:

1 Students with a variety of degrees of hearing loss, who use hearing aids, who have received an oral education, and whose first or preferred language is English, may require technical aids such as induction loops or infra red listening devices to support their learning.
2 Other students with similar levels of hearing loss and who have had similar educational experiences might prefer to work with the support of a lipspeaker, a notetaker, a speech-to-text operator or a combination of all three.
3 Students with a more severe or profound hearing loss may have been educated orally, in a total communication environment or in British Sign Language (BSL). They may be unable to, or choose not to, use hearing aids and may have chosen to use BSL as their first or preferred language. As a result, they might prefer to work with the support of a sign language interpreter, as well as a notetaker.
4 Others may choose different combinations of these different types of support dependent upon their specific needs and choices.

The essential point is that all of these forms of support, both human and mechanical, are media through which the message of education must pass if it is to reach the mind of the student. The level, content, clarity, accuracy and comprehensibility of the educational message received by the D/deaf student are wholly dependent upon the ability of these support media to function effectively.

So what are the characteristics of these different forms of support, and what effect might they be expected to have on the student's ability to access the message of the classroom, on the classroom environment, and on the other participants within that environment?

Mechanical aids

The ways in which mechanical aids provide for the access needs of the student are, on the whole, quite straightforward. Their function is to amplify or clarify sound, and provided that they are set up and working correctly they are expected to do so effectively. The difficulties that might arise are usually as a result of a lack of familiarity with the equipment and how it works on the part of those using it, or their lack of awareness of the needs of their D/deaf colleague or student. Such difficulties can arise particularly in settings where people are taking part in group or seminar work. Members of the group might forget to pass the microphone round, or might unconsciously tap the microphone or play with it. It is all too easy for this to happen, but such a lack of awareness in how to use the equipment appropriately can be both annoying and distracting for a D/deaf student, and, unless addressed, it can have a negative impact on their ability to learn (EDF 1996).

One thing, which occurs regularly in interpreting settings, including educational settings, and particularly in workshops and seminars, is the phenomenon of overlapping speech. This is where more than one person contributes simultaneously to the discussion or conversation (Brennan and Brown 1998). One of the natural functions of the ear is its ability to differentiate between a number of sounds and sound sources, allowing the brain to focus predominantly on one message while ignoring another. Mechanical amplifiers such as induction loops and hearing aids are not able to carry out this function, with the result that all sound is amplified to the same level (RNID 1998). As a result, a student accessing messages through the use of these devices is not able to filter and ignore the messages they receive in the same way as their hearing peers, and this again can cause them to miss or misunderstand information.

The use of mechanical aids in the classroom can have an effect not only on the learning experience of a D/deaf student, but on the other students and on the whole learning environment. It can be distracting to a Lecturer and other students in a classroom to have to pass around a microphone, or to wait to receive the microphone before they begin to speak. If nothing else, the spontaneity of the situation is dramatically altered. This is something which cannot be avoided if a D/deaf student is to be given an opportunity to access the classroom on an equal basis with their hearing peers, and is a direct result of the fact that the classroom, certainly in higher education institutions, is not designed specifically to meet the needs of a D/deaf student.

On the whole, while the mechanical aid might be seen as a simple solution which can restore or offer equal access for a deaf student, in reality it can have a significant effect on the learning experience not only of the D/deaf student, but of all involved.

Non-mechanical support, that which is provided by Human Aids to Communication (Panel of Four 1992), can be divided into two main categories: monolingual support and bilingual support.

Monolingual support workers

Monolingual support is, on the whole, the type of service that is provided by lipspeakers, notetakers and speech-to-text operators. These support workers would usually support a D/deaf student by providing communication in only one direction, from the originator (teacher, friend, fellow student, etc), and by changing the message from its original language mode (in our case spoken English) to another mode of the same language (English lip patterns, written English notes or English typed on a keyboard). The function of all of these workers is effectively transliteration, rather than translation or interpretation, since they change only to another mode of the language in which the message is given, rather than giving the message in a different language (CACDP 1998).

In addition, lipspeakers, notetakers and speech-to-text operators would not ordinarily expect to pass any message from the student back to the other participants. Rather, there would be an expectation that in such settings the student would communicate for him/herself.

The fact that this role is primarily carried out in only one direction and one language means that there is an expectation that the process can take place with little disruption or error. While this should be the case, the fact remains that to reach the student, a message must pass through these media. It could be said that to re-mouth words, or to write or type notes, an individual does not necessarily have to understand the original message, but it must be that case that, unless the message is clearly understood, it cannot be accurately passed on.

When writing notes, individuals often filter information, and write in a way that will remind them later of key points or concepts. Similarly, someone mouthing clearly the utterances of another may need to drop some linguistic elements in order to keep up with the original message. The effect in either case is that, before the message has reached the D/deaf student it may have been filtered and refined, and this is something over which the student him/herself has no control, and of which he/she may not even be aware.

Again, as with the use of mechanical aids, problems can be caused by the overlapping of speech. A lipspeaker can only re-mouth one message at a time, which means that where two or more utterances are happening simultaneously, they have to make a decision as to which utterance is most important or relevant to the student, and omit the other(s). Again it is the student who potentially misses out on information, and again this is something over which he/she has little, if any, control.

Bilingual support workers

The bilingual role is the one that is carried out by a sign language interpreter, and is the most complex of the processes which take place in supporting D/deaf students.

Unlike the roles of the monolingual workers, this entails two-way communication. The interpreter's role is to translate from a source language (in this case spoken English) to a different target language (BSL) (CACDP 1998). They are also expected to translate what is uttered by the student, in BSL, back into spoken English. This is a process of interpretation, rather than transliteration, since the interpreter is working into and out of two grammatically and structurally different languages.

The difficulties that have already been mentioned in connection with both technical and monolingual support for deaf students are equally if not more significant for those who provide an interpreting service. The very fact that an interpreter has to translate messages and concepts into a different language means that their need to comprehend the message is more significant than it is for the monolingual worker.

If an interpreter does not understand the content of a source message, they cannot be expected to accurately translate it into the target language (Frishberg 1990, Cokely 1992, Roy 1992). A consequence of this is that interpreters might be expected to have a certain degree of knowledge or understanding about the topic they are interpreting, and an awareness of the level at which the lecturer and the students are working.

The point that has just been made is not exclusive to educational interpreting. Whenever an interpreter is working between two languages it is essential that they have an understanding of the subject matter. In Educational settings, however, they might encounter particular issues because of the type of subject matter they are expected to deal with (Kluwin 1985).

An example of this is the difficulty that might arise out of the need to interpret poetry. Poetic language is, by its very nature, different from typical discourse. Often a poem uses obscure imagery, or a fixed meter. It is a frozen form, in the sense that its language, grammar and appearance on a page never change. The only variation might come about as a result of a reading or performance of that poem by an individual.

The difficulties facing an interpreter in this situation are many. They may need to be aware of the existence of a fixed form of the poem in BSL, and if one does exist, they would need to know and understand that BSL text in order to be able to perform it accurately. If no such translation or 'text' exists, they might face other problems. For example, how does one interpret a poem from 16th Century English into 20th Century BSL while remaining true to the form of the original? On another level, an interpreter may need to be aware of the intent of a lecturer in using this poem. Does the lecturer actually want a translation of the poem, or is it their intention to explain to the students the way in which meter is used. Does an interpreter show rhythm rather than content in their communication (Sanderson 1997)?

Another example of the complexity of the task might be an interpreter working in a lecture about Linguistics. The use of language to describe language, which the interpreter would be expected to undertake, could lead to all sorts of interpretation difficulties, especially for an interpreter who does not themselves fully understand linguistic issues (Harrington and Turner 1997).

It is true that, as a result of their own education, all interpreters will have some prior knowledge, at least of certain subjects. In particular they will have knowledge based on their own learning from the core primary and secondary curriculum which they encountered during their own schooling. In reality, however, the demands of post secondary knowledge that will be made of them when working in higher education will, in some cases at least, be beyond their ability and their personal experience (Johnson 1991).

A related issue is that of the language competence of an interpreter. Monolingual workers are working into and out of different modalities of one language. This language is their own first language and they are expected to be competent in all aspects of its use. Bilingual interpreters have to work into and out of two languages one of which (in most cases, BSL) is not native to them. There is an expectation that, in order to function effectively and accurately, an interpreter should be competent in both languages. If they do not have the lexical or grammatical knowledge to enable them to provide a competent or accurate interpretation, the student will not be able to access information effectively and will suffer as a consequence. So, in addition to being knowledgeable of the subject they are translating, interpreters are expected to have language skills to high levels in both the source and target languages.

Again, however, the issue is not simply one of language competence. We have already looked at some of the possible complexities of interpreting subject matter in higher education. In addition, there are complexities specific to the languages that are being used in these interpretations.

Most BSL/English interpreters expect to spend much of their time working from their first into their second language. Most of the lectures they will interpret will be given by an English speaking lecturer, and the target for that message will be a D/deaf student. It is entirely possible, however, that a lecture may be given by a Deaf tutor (Harrington 1998). In such cases, the interpretation is not being focused or tailored to the needs of one student, but rather is aimed at giving access to the majority. Even so, in such a situation, an interpreter could expect a Deaf lecturer to have prepared their presentation, and that they are used to presenting in front of students. As a result, the interpreter might expect to be working from a measured and structured delivery, and the issues should not be significantly different from any other lecture situation.

The situation can become more complex, however, when the presentation to be interpreted is being given by a student. The language used is likely to be different, the student is less likely to be an experienced presenter, and preparation may have been much more 'last minute'. An interpreter may feel less pressured when the recipient of their interpretation is a single D/deaf student, although this sense of pressure is likely to increase when the presenter is a D/deaf BSL user, and the audience is a group of hearing students (Winston 1997, Harrington 1998).

Another issue for the interpreter is the way in which they may need, or be forced by circumstances, to filter the message. The process of interpreting demands that the interpreter works with a time lag, which means that they have to hear and understand a message before they can begin to translate it. While listening to a message and operating such a time lag, interpreters are constantly making choices about how they carry out the translation of that message. If an interpreter does not understand part of a message, or if a message is too fast, they may opt to drop or omit some elements of it. Again, the manner in which a message is translated, the lexical choices and grammatical decisions that interpreters take, can all lead to some nuances of the original message being lost or altered. This may not be conscious omission, and it is certainly not the intention of an interpreter to deliberately mislead or misinform a student, but it can naturally occur as part of the interpreting process, particularly as the interpretation happens simultaneously.

It is fair to suggest, therefore, that, during the communication process that has been described, a D/deaf student using the services of an interpreter receives a message only after it has passed through the mind of that interpreter. The student may be unaware that anything has been omitted or changed, and they certainly have little if any control over the decisions made by the interpreter to filter or omit part of that message.

Again, where there is overlapping speech, the interpreter has to take decisions about which utterance is of greatest significance to the student, with the possibility that the student will miss at least some part of the entire interaction.

Finally there is another issue for the bilingual interpreter that arises from the fact that BSL, unlike English or any other spoken language, is a visual-gestural language rather than an oral-aural language. The visual nature of the language means that it can be much more difficult for an interpreter to ask a question of a deaf student without giving away the answer. A simple example of this can be seen in the following question: 'how many sides does a triangle have?' The fact that an interpreter actually has to draw a triangle in the air as an integral part of their translation means that they give the answer away as they ask the question.

To deal appropriately with these issues, one would expect that interpreters working in educational settings would be among the most highly qualified and experienced. In reality, certainly in the UK at the present time, this is not always the case.

Training and qualifications of interpreters

The training, registration and qualification of interpreters are currently in the process of being revised in the UK. The examinations for advanced level language skills, known as stage III, and for qualification as an interpreter, known as the registered qualified sign language interpreter (RQSLI) examination, have recently been replaced by National Vocational Qualifications (NVQ) at level three and level four. The Council for the Advancement of Communication with Deaf People (CACDP) has been responsible both for the old assessments and the introduction of the new NVQ assessments. CACDP also offers sign language qualifications at stage I (elementary) and stage II (intermediate), as well as qualifications in lipspeaking, deafblind communication and deaf awareness (CACDP 1998).

CACDP currently administers two levels of registration for interpreters. Those who are qualified (RQI) become members of the Register of sign language interpreters, but there is also a register for those who have passed stage III, are on a recognised training course and are working towards qualification. These interpreters are known as registered trainee interpreters (RTI). There is currently only one category of trainee, although it is likely that CACDP's revised policy will introduce two categories to differentiate those who have recently commenced training from those whose training is nearing completion, and who have higher levels of skill and experience.

There are a variety of available routes to qualification for interpreters. Some are based in universities, either full time or part time, while others are provided by independent training organisations. There is currently a single national Register for interpreters, and it is expected that the development of NVQ standards will lead to the establishment of a single national benchmark qualification for interpreters. The Register is currently administered by CACDP, and, regardless of which training course an individual has attended, they apply to CACDP for membership of the Register.

In 1997, as part of an ongoing project in the University of Central Lancashire, looking at access to education for D/deaf students using interpreters, questionnaires were sent out to all qualified and trainee interpreters to find out whether or not they worked in educational settings in the country, a total of 295 individuals. There were two purposes to the questionnaire:

1 To find out whether these interpreters were working regularly in Higher education.
2 To find out what levels of qualification these interpreters had attained for themselves.

The reason for this second question is that as has been suggested already, to interpret well in a higher education setting, an interpreter needs to have an appropriate level of knowledge and understanding of the HE setting, as well as bilingual and interpreting skills.

The return rate for the survey was 57.7%, and the results confirmed that a vast majority of qualified and trainee interpreter in the UK (more than 85%) do not undertake any regular interpreting assignments in higher education settings. It must be the case, then, that much of the higher education interpreting is being carried out by people who have not trained or qualified as interpreters, and who do not possess the minimum required language competence level to commence interpreter training.

One reason for this is that educational interpreting is comparatively poorly paid, and while qualified interpreters can command much higher fees for undertaking assignments in the legal profession, in medical settings, and in theatre and television, there is no incentive for them to take educational work. Added to this, there is a general lack of qualified interpreters at present. When the survey of interpreters was taken in 1997, there were only 143 RQIs in the whole of England, Wales and Northern Ireland. It is not surprising, then, that much of the educational interpreting is left to people with lower levels of skill, who do not charge as much, and who are unable, or choose not, to undertake other more high profile interpreting jobs.

Many of these unqualified interpreters may have followed a course of training which leads to a certificate in communication support work (CSW). The role of communication support worker is unique to the UK and was established in the late 1980s with Government funding to train individuals who could support young D/deaf people on government training schemes such as the youth training scheme (YTS) or the employment training scheme (ET).

The Rise of the Communicator (Green and Nickerson 1992) describes the aim of communicator training as follows:

> "… to train hearing people to a level of skills in communicating with deaf people, accompanied by an appropriate understanding of their needs, so as to enable them to gain employment as YTS or ET communicators, social work assistants, residential care assistants in schools for deaf children, etc., where communication skills, not teaching skills, are paramount."

When it was first established, communicator training was designed in such a way that it would enable people with no prior knowledge of sign language to attain stage III in one year. After the initial course had run for three years, the same model was established in a number of colleges of further education around the country, but the sign language exit level was reduced to stage II. It is now more than ten years since communicator training was first established, and in that time there have been no significant changes to the entry requirements, exit levels or curriculum.

The one thing that has changed, however, is the status given to the CSW qualification by those who employ educational interpreters. As Green and Nickerson (1992) said, it was designed to train people to a level at which they might support young D/deaf people on government training schemes. Without significant changes to the curriculum or the expected exit skill levels of those who undertake it, it is becoming apparent that this training is accepted by many as an appropriate qualification for those who support students in education at all levels, from nursery school to higher education.

So the expectations in terms of ability, knowledge and educational background for interpreters working in higher education are set high. However, in reality, those providing bilingual support to D/deaf students may, in some cases at least, be doing so without appropriate levels of linguistic skill, interpreter training, knowledge of the subject with which they are working or personal experience of the higher education sector.

Conclusions

The first and overriding concern of those who are responsible for assessing the needs of D/deaf students, and providing for those needs, is that of identifying and supplying the required support services, either mechanical or human. To this end, it is understandable that significant amounts of the work that has been carried out in recent times, investigating the needs of such students, have been focused on the funding and provision of services, rather than on their effectiveness. Provision on its own, however, does not provide equality of access for the D/deaf student. There are a whole host of factors at play, of which we can only become aware once the provision is in place, and the learning environment itself is looked at. It is these that need to be addressed if we are to give D/deaf students an opportunity to access higher education on a fair and equal footing with their hearing peers.

The demands of an ideal world for D/deaf students in higher education would be that we provide them with guaranteed support that would not hamper their ability to learn. In terns of interpreting support, we might expect this to be provided by truly bilingual interpreters with high levels of skill in both source and target languages. Interpreters might be expected to have personal experience of the learning environment and its demands, ideally through having undergone their own study in a higher education environment. They might be expected to have knowledge and understanding of the subject/s that they are interpreting, and ideally they should have undergone some specialist training in educational interpreting in higher education institutions.

The reality of the situation in the UK at present is that few, if any, D/deaf students are going to be provided with the services of an interpreter who meets these high demands. As has been said, many qualified interpreters do not accept work in educational settings, for many reasons, and as a result, those with lower interpreting skills, lower qualifications and less interpreting experience are the ones who provide much of the support that is offered to D/deaf students. Although it was never intended to be a qualification for supporting students in higher education, the Edexcel Communication Support Worker qualification is the only one that currently trains people specifically who work with D/deaf students. It is true that, in addition, some interpreter training courses include a module on educational interpreting, but there is currently no dedicated course to train interpreters to work with D/deaf students in higher education in this country.

In reality then, those providing support for D/deaf students are left with some difficulties. They may have to provide imperfect services, using unqualified or under-qualified interpreters. However, as long as they are aware that these limitations can cause problems for the student and the learning environment, they should be able to use the available resources to their best advantage. In doing so, and while the services they provide will not be perfect, they should be able to meet the needs of the student by at least providing a service. They can try to engage the best services available, even though this may not always be possible. They can try to ensure that preparation materials are always available for the interpreter, and can provide role awareness for lecturers and students, in an attempt to minimise the negative effect of the non-deaf classroom on the D/deaf student.

It is also essential, however, that in providing for the reality, we do not lose sight of the ideals. Things will only improve in the future if we accept the challenge and embrace the issues that currently prevent us from allowing D/deaf students equal access to the curriculum.

References

Barnes, L. 1996. higher education and the Deaf Student: Widening Access or Limiting Participation. Paper given at The Dilemmas of Mass higher education, International Conference. Staffordshire University, 10 April 1996.

Brennan, M. and Brown, R. 1998. *Equality before the Law: Deaf People's Access to Justice.* DSRU, Durham University: Durham

CACDP (1998). *Directory.* CACDP: Durham.

Cokely, D. 1990. The Effectiveness of Three Means of Communication in the College Classroom. In *Sign Language Studies, 69,* 415–442.

—— 1992. *Sign Language Interpreting and Interpreters.* Linstock Press: Burtonsville, MD.

European Disability Forum (EDF) 1996. *Towards the Equalisation of Opportunities for Disabled People: Into the Mainstream?* SEDDP: Brussels.

Ellwood, J. and Webster, A. 1986. *The Hearing Impaired Child in the Ordinary School.* Croom Helm: London, Sydney and Wolfeboro.

Frishberg, N. 1990. *Interpreting: an Introduction* RID, Silver Spring, Maryland.

Green, C. and Nickerson, W. 1992. *The Rise of the Communicator: a Perspective on Post-16 Education and Training for Deaf People.* Moonshine Books: England.

Harrington, F.J. 1998. (2000) Sign Language Interpreters and Access for Deaf Students to University Curricula: The Ideal and the Reality, in: Roberts, R., Carr, S.A., Abraham, D. and Dufour, A. (eds) *The Critical Link 2: Interpreters in the community.* Benjamins Translation Library, 31.

John Benjamin: Holland.

Harrington F.J. and Turner, G.H. 1997. Making Language Work—Interpreting the Curriculum with Deaf Students. Paper given at the BAAL Annual Conference, Birmingham, September 1997.

Johnson, K. 1991. Miscommunication in Interpreted Classroom Interaction. In *Sign Language Studies*, 70.

Kluwin, T.N. 1985. The Acquisition of Content from a Signed Lecture. In *Sign Language Studies*, 48, 269–286.

Panel of Four, 1992 *Communication is Your Responsibility: the Commission of Enquiry into Human Aids to Communication* John Knight: England

Royal National Institute for Deaf People (RNID) 1998 *Factsheet: Hearing Aids* RNID: London.

Roy, C.B. 1992. A Sociolinguistic Analysis of the Interpreter's Role in Simultaneous Talk in a Face to Face Interpreted Dialogue. In *Sign Language Studies*, 74.

Sanderson, G. 1997. Developing Your Own IEP. Paper given at the National Educational Interpreters Conference, Long Beach, California, August 3, 1997.

Winston, E. 1994. An Interpreted Education: inclusion or exclusion? In Johnson, R.C. and Cohen, O.P. *Implications and Complications for deaf Students of the Full Inclusion Movement*. Gallaudet Research Institute Occasional Paper 94–2. Gallaudet University: Washington, DC.

—— 1997. Interpreting in the Classroom: Providing Accessibility or Creating New Barriers. Paper given at the National Educational Interpreters Conference, Long Beach, California, August 3, 1997.

The rise, fall and re-invention of the communicator: re-defining roles and responsibilities in educational interpreting

Frank J. Harrington

Abstract

In 1987, the first (pilot) training course for communicators in further education was established, "to train hearing people to a level of skills in communicating with deaf people, accompanied by an appropriate understanding of their needs, so as to enable them to gain employment as YTS or ET communicators" (Green and Nickerson 1992). Fourteen years on, this same training is now seen as an appropriate qualification for hearing people working as communicators, and carrying out a myriad of different support roles, with deaf children and students in primary, secondary, further and higher education settings.

This paper will explore the origins of the communicator. It will also, in light of the complexities of the modern day task of supporting students in a variety of educational settings, discuss the communicator's various roles and functions. It will discuss the merits of continuing (or not) to use multi-tasking individuals to provide for the various and complex needs of deaf students in educational settings, and whether, in future, deaf students might be better, or more appropriately, served by a number of skilled individual carrying out single support functions.

Introduction

The title *Communication Support Worker* (CSW) in education is used to describe a role that is unique to the UK. In the mid-1980s the role was defined, and training established, to take advantage of government funding which became available through the Manpower Services Commission (MSC), and which was intended to provide greater employment opportunities for disabled people through employment training programmes. An increasing number of young deaf British Sign Language (BSL) users were being enrolled on these programmes, and in their case, MSC funding was used to train people who could provide

Keynote paper given at *Supporting Deaf People*: An International Online Conference for Interpreting Professionals, 3 June 2001 them with communication support and greater access. The funding was used to establish a two-year pilot communicator training initiative, run first at Bourneville College, Birmingham, and later Coventry Technical College, in collaboration with Birmingham Institute for the Deaf. At the end of the first two years, the training continued to run as the Coventry (ECSTRA) communicator's course, and became the blueprint for communicator training courses now running in colleges across the country. (Green and Nickerson 1992:117ff)

According to Green and Nickerson, the role of the communicator was defined and developed during the mid-1980s at a series of NATED workshops, the last of which met in Coventry in 1985. One major outcome of that final workshop was a report which listed the sources and types of support that were felt to be required by deaf students entering post-compulsory education. The list included: interpreter; lip-speaker; social worker; teacher of the deaf; note-taker; personal tutor; counsellor among others (Green and Nickerson 1992, p65).

Students requiring these various types of support needed to be served by a number of professionals who were appropriately trained to deliver different elements.

"This approach must have a properly constituted team that could carry out initial and on-going assessment, and provide a proper support base for individual students whilst maintaining a working liaison with all concerned. The team or teams would also require a Manager for the most efficient use of resources" (Green and Nickerson 1992:69)

This quotation (taken from the report of the 1985 NATED workshop) shows clearly that NATED members believed that the needs of deaf students were complex, requiring the support of a multi-skilled, multi-disciplined, managed team. However, the financial and time constraints within which they were working at that time ensured that such teams were an ideal to be aspired to, rather than an attainable reality (Green and Nickerson 1992:72).

Crucially, as NATED and others strove to develop, and provide, at least some elements of the required support identified by the 1985 workshop, they found themselves moving away from individuals and their the roles, focussing instead on defining the 'functions' that would provide the support students needed. Once the individual skill elements of the team service were defined as functions, it was much easier to consider the notion that single individuals could be trained to carry out a number of these functions. It was ultimately quite an easy step to replace the 'team' with an individual, the communicator. Just seven years on from the 1985 NATED workshop, Green and Nickerson were describing the role of the individual communicator working in further education as fulfilling the functions of interpreter, language tutor, note-taker and top-up teacher all at once (Green and Nickerson 1992:182).

The communicator training itself was targeted at young people who were unemployed and who had no post-secondary qualifications (this was a requirement in order for individual students to qualify for MSC funding). It was also designed to enable these students to attain CACDP stage III (advanced communication skills) within one year. The aim of communicator training was:

> "to train hearing people to a level of skills in communicating with deaf people, accompanied by an appropriate understanding of their needs, so as to enable them to gain employment as YTS or ET communicators, social work assistants, residential care assistants in schools for deaf children, etc." (Green and Nickerson 1992:120)

This aim was quite specific, and limited, in terms of what communicator training was expected to achieve. The primary focus was the development of language competence, with some knowledge of other support strategies to identify, and in some way meet, the needs of those being supported. Interpreting, teaching and other skills were also touched on to a greater or lesser degree in the training, but students completing the course did not hold high-level qualifications in any of these disciplines.

Although an additional (optional) module focusing on higher education has recently been developed, the training that CSWs receive today has, otherwise, not changed significantly (Harrington 1998, Pickersgill 2000). Yet, ten years on from Green and Nickerson, CSWs are expected to fulfill a number of diverse and complex needs for those with whom they work, needs which differ significantly from one setting to another. The CSW qualification, originally intended as a foundation course (Green and Nickerson 1992:153) to train support workers for young deaf adults in employment training programmes, is now seen by many employers in education as an appropriate qualification for anyone undertaking any form of support work with deaf students in Primary, Secondary, Tertiary and Higher education settings.

Information available suggests that entry criteria for CSW courses are not standardized. Some institutions insist that students have Stage III signing skills when entering the programme; others expect their students to have attained this level by the end of the course. However, a significant number of institutions offering CSW qualifications will take students with Stage II, (or the capacity to pass Stage II—i.e. holding Stage I) and so in some cases there is no guarantee that people following the course will have attained signing skills higher than Stage II by the time they finish. In most cases, the academic requirement for entry to the course is 5 GCSEs. So it is clear that, while the range and complexity of the roles that CSWs are expected to undertake have increased, the required and expected level of language attainment by those taking on these roles has, in some cases at least, been significantly lowered.

There are historical reasons why CSWs carry out a number of different roles, and it is not my intention to denigrate in any way those who have been trained and who work as CSWs. However, in the interest of service users (deaf children, deaf young people and deaf adults in education) I am not convinced that the roles carried out by CSWs can appropriately remain the responsibility of one individual, or that the training available to them at present adequately prepares them for all of the tasks they undertake.

The CSW as educational interpreter?

In recent years, the Council for the Advancement of Communication with Deaf People (CACDP) has focused much of its energy into the establishment of guidelines, regulations and standards relating to Sign language Interpreters. Who is an interpreter? What qualifications should someone hold in order to call themselves an interpreter? What sort of assignments are non-qualified interpreters allowed to carry out, and in what circumstances?

Decisions that have been taken, and guidelines that have been established in answer to these and other questions, have led to an accepted understanding of the role and function of the interpreter. There has been a general acceptance of the levels of linguistic ability required of someone who wishes to work as an interpreter, and a Code of Ethics and complaints procedure have been developed in an attempt to ensure that deaf people receive, where possible, a consistent basic standard of service.

We have already seen that the work CSWs are expected to do, because of their multiple roles, is more complex than that of the interpreter. They are expected at times to note-take, to be a teaching aide, and to provide all kinds of support to the students with whom they work, in addition to providing a translation and interpreting service. They function in a wide variety of educational settings, and with Deaf people ranging from young children to adults. They are not necessarily expected to work only in English and BSL, but may also need to be able to switch between a number of versions of manually coded English (MCE) as well, dependent upon the needs of the individual deaf student with whom they are working.

But regardless of where it is that they work, or the age of the student they are supporting, the majority of them spend a large proportion of their time functioning as interpreters. In other words, it is one of their primary functions, every day, to take a message in a source language, whether that be written or spoken English, or any variety of Sign Language, comprehend it, translate it using the correct structure and vocabulary and produce it accurately in the target language required by the person needing the interpretation. The information that CSWs are being asked to interpret is often complex, especially in higher education situations, and, because of the nature of education, it is almost always information with which the student is not completely familiar (Cokeley 1990, Johnson 1991, and Roy 1992).

Every interpretation is an example of language use by the interpreter. Interpreting, therefore, affects every aspect of an interpreted education. In any educational setting, the teacher's language and the student's language are only accessible in combination with the interpreter's language (Winston 1994, 1997), so it follows that the language competence and interpreting skills of the interpreter are essential to the success of the educational experience.

In a three year project carried out at the University of Central Lancashire (UCLAN), over 30 hours of interpreted classroom interaction were observed, and amongst the many findings, the project team identified an interpreter's language competence and interpreting ability as being of primary importance in order for the educational event to be successful (Harrington 2000).

Anyone performing the task of interpreter in education on a regular basis should reasonably be expected, not only to be highly skilled in both English and BSL, but also to have a working knowledge of the subject(s) which they are being asked to translate. If they are working in post-compulsory education, they should also have a degree, or at least some personal experience of studying in similar educational settings to those in which they are working.

The UCLAN research project found that only 10% of qualified interpreters, and 13% of trainee interpreter undertook any regular educational interpreting work. Most of those who did were working in FE or HE. It is clear then, that most educational interpreting, and particularly almost all of the work being done in compulsory education with the youngest deaf children, is being undertaken by people who have lower language skills and who are less likely to have undergone any formal interpreter training.

Educational interpreting has long been looked down upon by the interpreting profession in this country. The reason that most qualified and trainee interpreters don't accept educational interpreting work is: because it is poorly paid, because those who undertake the work are not expected to have high level qualifications, and because there has been confusion about additional responsibilities they will be expected to take on. It has been suggested that many aspiring interpreters have taken communicator training courses and educational interpreting work as a stepping stone towards becoming qualified and registered as interpreters (Green and Nickerson 1992:185). But is it right that, just because this part of the interpreting profession is afforded a lower kudos, and lower pay, we should accept, or even expect a lower standard of service?

To use an analogy drawn by Mark Heaton and David Fowler (1997), one has the right to choose interpreters, just as one has the right to choose which form of aspirin they might use. Some aspirins are soluble, others are in tablet form, some are formulated for young children, and so on. One always chooses the medication most appropriate for the requirements of the individual, but if the powder, tablet or syrup does not contain the right amount of aspirin it won't cure the pain. In the same way, some interpreters function better in court, in hospital or in education, but if they don't have the language skills, then no matter where they function, they cannot do so effectively.

Communicators courses are not recognised by CACDP or ay other body as interpreter training courses, and CACDP has itself gone to great lengths to stress that a Stage II, or even Stage III certificate is not an interpreting qualification. If a major part of the communicator's role is interpreting, it is a task for which many of them may not be adequately skilled, trained or qualified at present.

It may be that, having followed a communicators course, CSW's are better prepared to carry out the functions of aide, note-taker, lip-speaker, etc., than qualified interpreters who have not been through CSW training. Even so, the ability to function effectively in these roles demands advanced knowledge and experience of not only the subject matter, but also the setting in which they are working. If we take higher education as an example, someone who has never attended a college or university cannot be expected to understand the 'culture' of such a setting, how it functions, or the demands of the language used by those who teach and study at that level.

It has been argued that Deaf students in colleges or schools do not have high levels of language skill, and that they can, therefore, be served by someone whose own language skills are more basic. Winston's (1994, 1997) view is that the presence of an interpreter assumes that everyone involved in the interpreted event has language competence. A deaf student is not supposed to be learning language in the classroom, they are supposed to be learning content. Similarly then, an interpreter is not supposed to be practising language skills in the classroom, they are supposed to be interpreting content.

In the school classroom, unless there is a Deaf support worker, the CSW is often the only sign language role model. It has been suggested (Sanderson 1997, Winston 1994, 1997) that it might be far more sensible for the linguistically most qualified people (i.e. deaf classroom support professionals whose first language is BSL, or at least fully qualified interpreters) were to work with the youngest children. This would give deaf students the opportunity to maximise their use of language in the classroom, rather than being in a situation where they might be better skilled linguistically than the person supporting them.

Understanding the domains, separating the roles

I have already suggested that a principal role of the CSW is that of interpreter. Scholars both in this country and abroad (Winston 1994, 1997, O'Neill, Perry and Pickersgill 1999, Pickersgill 2000) have suggested that the interpreting role and other roles carried out by those who provide communication support in education should be separated out, and perhaps even cease to be the responsibility of a single individual.

Winston (1994, 1997) identified three roles that are often expected of the interpreter in mainstream educational settings.

Interpretation: the transmission, from one language to another, of other people's information.

Tutoring: transmitting information outside of the interpreting role.

Aide: carrying out other duties related to the educational setting.

She strongly suggests that of these, the second and third should not necessarily be seen as the responsibility of someone whose primary function is to interpret. It may be that everyone working in a particular setting takes on some of the 'aide' tasks (playground duty, bus queue duty, etc), and therefore an interpreter employed by a particular school or college might also be asked to do these. The 'tutor' role is definitely seen by Winston to be a separate role, requiring separate skills and training.

In reports of a project carried for CACDP, Pickersgill (2000) and O'Neill et al (1999) make a clear distinction between what they refer to as *monolingual* and *bilingual* support roles in education.

The monolingual roles referred to include lip-speaking, note-taking and language support, all of which demand that an individual work between different modes of a single language. The lip-speaker works from spoken English to mouthed, silent English lip pattern. The note taker works from spoken English to written English, while the language support tutor works from one form of written English to another. Each of these is a skill that requires practice and training. The lip-speaker and note-taker may need subject specific knowledge, while a language support tutor might need to be a trained teacher, or even teacher of the deaf.

The bilingual role is the same as that which was described above as the interpreter role. Given what we know of the interpreting profession, training and qualifications, it follows that, if the bilingual role is separated out from the other roles of the CSW, then those working as interpreters in education should be trained and qualified to the same levels as those who interpret in other settings.

If we take these suggestions to their possible conclusions, we might find ourselves drawing a very different picture of language mediation and support in education at all levels.

In primary education it might be difficult to separate out the roles in the ways we might want to later on. However, we might want to see teachers in the classroom being supported first and foremost by a native BSL user (a language role model) who has experience and training as a teacher. Perhaps we might even want to see deaf teachers taking the lead in giving the youngest children access to all aspects of their education, and thus a solid educational foundation, in their first language, BSL.

In secondary education we might want to see separate individuals taking on the role of interpreter/lip-speaker, language support tutor, study aide and note-taker, all working in partnership with the teacher. They could all be seen as tools that the teacher must use, but it would remain the responsibility of the teacher to do the teaching, not anyone else. It is not the job of an interpreter to make a deaf student learn the subject. Rather it is the aim of the interpreter to make the subject accessible (Winston 1994, 1997).

An interpreter cannot be expected to bridge the gap created by lack of cognitive ability on the part of the deaf student. Maybe this is the role that might be taken on by a study aide or personal tutor, who might be expected to have appropriate language skills, subject specific knowledge and a teaching qualification.

A language support tutor might work on second language (English) development, particularly in relation to written English, with a student if and when this were required (O'Neill 1999).

A note-taker might be available for a student to have written notes for reference and revision, and again, this person would need to be trained. They would certainly need to have written English skills beyond 'A' level standard in order to meet the needs of older students.

All of these roles would require training, skills and abilities which may not necessarily be found in a single person. Furthermore, there may be times when two or more of these roles are required at the same time, making it impossible for one person to provide them adequately or appropriately.

In further education it is suggested that we might expect to see similar divisions of labour as in secondary education, and for similar reasons.

In higher education we already see some of these distinctions being made, with separate people taking on the role of interpreter, note-taker and language support tutor, and receiving separate, specialist training before undertaking these roles. It is certainly not the case that this happens throughout the HE sector, but at last the precedent is being set (Harrington 2000, Smith 1997).

I accept that these suggestions may seem idealistic, and in some instances far from achievable. However, it is becoming clear that some of them at least need to be considered if our deaf children and young deaf adults are going to have any real chance of surviving in a speech-based education system which is not designed to meet their needs (Stewart and Kluwin 1996, Hayes 1992, Brennan 1999).

CACDP has begun to explore issues of regulation and registration for CSWs, while Edexcel, the awarding body for CSW qualifications, has begun to develop a course to train deaf teaching assistants. But these initiatives, in isolation, will not necessarily help to clarify the overall situation.

The Association of Sign Language Interpreters (ASLI) recently published a draft code of practice for educational interpreters and employers (ASLI 2001). Again, while there is no problem in an organisation such as ASLI devising a policy for itself on interpreting in education, such a policy cannot be successfully introduced (or enforced) outside of the organisation without the co-operation and endorsement of employers, educators, trainers, CSWs (who, because of their understanding of the roles they fulfil, may not wish to call themselves educational interpreters at this stage), and deaf students.

There are many issues that need to be addressed. The status and purpose of the various functions of the CSW need to be re-defined and re-valued. If we suggest that these various functions need to be carried out by separately skilled and more highly trained individuals, there are enormous implications in terms of cost, not to mention the need for a complete change of philosophy, for educators and employers.

If any change is going to be effected, it will be essential for all of the stakeholders (awarding bodies, deaf organisations, training organisations, professional associations, and individuals) to be involved in the process on an equal basis from the beginning. Different groups of stakeholders will have different agendas and different priorities, and these will need to be heard and shared if progress is to be made.

It may take a long time to bring about any change. Some changes may never happen, but one thing is becoming increasingly clear. The communicator of Green and Nickerson cannot continue to meet all of the educational needs of the modern deaf student in the current education system. If we do no more than embrace the idea that change is necessary, we will have begun the process that may make such change a reality.

References

ASLI (2001) Code of Practice for Educational Interpreters and Draft Guidelines for Employers of Educational Interpreters, in *Looksli*, 4.

Brennan, M. (1999) Challenging Linguistic Exclusion in Deaf Education in *Deaf Worlds* 15/1.

Cokeley, D. (1990) The Effectiveness of Three Means of Communication in the College Classroom in *Sign Language Studies*, 69.

Green, C. and Nickerson, W. (1992) *The Rise of the Communicator*. Moonshine Books: England.

Harrington, F.J. (1998) Issues Relating to the Possible Establishment of a Register of Communication Support Workers in *NEWSLI*, 32.

―― (2000) Sign Language Interpreters and Access for Deaf Students to University Curricula: The Ideal and the Reality, in: Roberts, R., Carr, S.A., Abraham, D. and Dufour, A. (eds) *The Critical Link 2: Interpreters* in the community. Benjamins Translation Library, 31. John Benjamin: Holland.

Hayes, P.L. (1992) Educational Interpreters for Deaf Students: Their Responsibilities, Problems and Concerns in *Journal of interpretation*, 5/1.

Heaton, M. and Fowler, D. (1997) Aches, Aspirins and Aspirations: A Deaf perspective on interpreting service delivery in *Deaf Worlds*, 13/3.

Johnson, K. (1991) Miscommunication in Interpreted Classroom Interaction in *Sign Language Studies*, 70.

O'Neill, R. (1999) Is Literacy Necessary? In *Deaf Worlds*, 15/2.

O'Neill, R., Perry, B. and Pickersgill, M. (1999) Recommendations Regarding the Future Training, Qualification and Registration of Communication Support Workers in Education: report of the CACDP advisory group. Unpublished report presented to CACDP, March 1999.

Pickersgill, M. (2000) Update on recommendations Regarding the Future Training, Qualification and Registration of Communication Support Workers in Education. Unpublished report presented to CACDP, October 2000.

Roy, C.B. (1992) A Sociolinguistic Analysis of the Interpreter's Role in Simultaneous Talk in a Face-to-Face Interpreted Dialogue in *Sign language Studies*, 74.

Sanderson, G. (1997) Developing your own I.E.P. Paper given at the National Educational Interpreting Conference, Long Beach, CA, August 3 1997.

Smith, A. (1997) Supporting the Learning of deaf students in higher education: a case study at Sheffield Hallam University in Journal of Further and higher education, 21/3.

Stewart, D.A. and Kluwin, T.N. (1996) The gap between Guidelines, Practice and Knowledge in Interpreting Services for Deaf Students in Journal of Deaf Studies and Deaf Education 1/ 1.

Winston, E.A. (1994) An Interpreted Education: Inclusion or Exclusion? in Johnson, R.C. and Cohen, O.P. (Eds.) Implications and Complications for Deaf Students of the Full Inclusion Movement. Gallaudet Research Institute Occasional Paper 94/2. Gallaudet University: Washington D.C.

——(1997) Interpreting in the Classroom: Providing Accessibility or Creating New Barriers? Paper given at the National Educational Interpreting Conference, Long Beach, CA, August 3, 1997.

3
ANALYSES OF INTERPRETING PRACTICES
Health & social care

Deaf women: informed choice, policy and legislation
Ros Bramwell, Frank J. Harrington and Jennifer Harris

Abstract

The maternity care of Deaf women is a subject which has received little attention, either within midwifery research, or within the arena of disability studies. Previous research has highlighted basic difficulties of access and information for such women. Midwives need to be aware of the challenges which can exist in ensuring Deaf women can give informed consent, and that their rights and expectations under the Patients' Charter and Disability Discrimination Act are met. Failure of communication could potentially lead to a civil action for negligence. The use of relatives and friends for translation is still a common practice, but a case study illustrates the way in which this can distort even a relatively straightforward communication. Increasingly, the threat of litigation will probably lead to a growth in the availability of professional sign language interpreters, but maternity services may wish to consider the relative merits of different models for accessing these services.[1]

Introduction

The maternity care of Deaf women is a subject which has received insufficient attention, either within midwifery research, or within the arena of disability studies. The literature which exists for the most part touches upon the very basic issues such as access difficulties and inadequate information (Thomas and Curtis 1997). Shackle (1994) came to similar conclusions in her study of 199 parents with disabilities.

While such studies are valuable for the ground-breaking manner in which they have put the issues of negative attitudes towards disabled parents squarely on the map, they make two assumptions concerning Deaf women.

First, there is an assumption that deafness should be treated as a disability for the purposes of designing and implementing services. As we have noted however, in a previous article (Bramwell *et al*, 2000), deaf people do not generally consider themselves disabled and in particular, British Sign Language users are more comfortable with linguistic minority status.

Second, the emphasis upon issues of physical access (such as adequate space in delivery suites for wheelchairs) given in these studies, are not as important to Deaf women as other issues, such as the appropriateness of the means of communicating with midwives.

In this article we set out the case for a discussion of these issues and focus particularly upon the issue of informed choice before moving to a discussion of the policy and legislative frameworks.

Informed consent

Changing Childbirth (Expert Maternity Group, 1993) formed a landmark in the move towards greater choice and autonomy for women in pregnancy and childbirth, and this brought with it a greater awareness of the need for women to have information on which to base choice and consent.

The importance of communication and information in maternity care is also made explicit in *Changing Childbirth*, which has as one of its objectives that 'information about maternity services should be provided in a form appropriate and accessible to women'. Indeed the needs of Deaf women are highlighted in part II (Survey of Good Communications Practice) of the report.

The importance of informed consent in the midwife's role is explained in the *Guidelines for Professional Practice* (UKCC 1996). Section 28 points out that the potential consequence, if the client feels that the information they received was insufficient, is a legal action for negligence. The guidelines for good practice make it clear that:

> "The... client's decision whether or not to agree to treatment must be based on adequate information... it is important that this information is shared freely with the... client, in an accessible way... It is important that you give the information in... (an) understandable way and that you give the... client enough time to ask questions if they wish."

All of this makes clear the central role that good communication plays in underpinning informed consent. This is covered in the section (22) of the guidelines on communication, which specifically states:

> "You may need the services of interpreters to make sure that information is understood."

The Patients' Charter

The Patients' Charter, as with other elements of the Citizens' Charter, was written as an equal opportunities statement for the Health Service. As such, it makes a number of suggestions and recommendations as to the quality and level of services members of the public have the right to, or can expect to receive. The first distinction is made between 'Rights' and 'Expectations'.

A 'Right' is something 'which all patients will receive all the time'; and an 'expectation' is a "standard of service which the NHS is aiming to achieve" (NHS 1995). There are particular statements which, when applied to deaf people as members of a disabled group, can have enormous implications in terms of the communication support with which they might expect to be provided. The Charter states that:

> "you can expect the NHS to make it easy for everyone to use its services, including children, elderly people or people with physical or mental disabilities." (Section 1: Access to Services)

While this section is intended to focus primarily on physical access, Deaf people will have needs which relate specifically to access to information, and as a result will expect the issue of communication to be dealt as part of this policy. Under the heading 'Providing Information' the Charter goes on to point out that individuals have the right to:

> "have any proposed treatment, including any risks involved in that treatment and any alternatives clearly explained to you before you decide whether to agree to it".

Given the charter's position on access, and the fact that a right is something that a person will receive all the time, Deaf people should expect to be provided with appropriate communication support in any consultation, and at any time when their treatment is being explained to them.

In addition, the Charter states that any individual can expect "friends and relatives to be kept up to date with the progress of your treatment" (Section 4: Your care in hospital). Where the relatives and carers are themselves Deaf, there will be an additional expectation that all such information sharing and consultation will also take place through the services of an appropriately skilled interpreter.

Implications for practice

In reality, many practitioners in both primary and secondary healthcare settings are not always fully aware of the implications of these sections of the Patients' Charter. Many health professionals have, in the past, seen the use of relatives and children of Deaf people as appropriate communicators in such settings, but as has been shown, this is not necessarily good or recommended practice for a number of reasons (Harrington 1998).

Often relatives, and especially children, will be emotionally involved in the situation. In addition, they simply may not understand the full implications of the message they are trying to translate, and in most cases they will not have received any training as interpreters, nor, more significantly, specific training to interpret in medical settings.

Put simply, this is not only inappropriate, but an unsafe practice, and in the case of children, might even be seen as abusive. John Bowis, former Under-Secretary of State for Health commented in 1993 at a public meeting held to discuss the implications for the health authority of the document *Communication is Your Responsibility: Report of the Commission of Enquiry into Human Aids to Communication* (1992) that:

> "We should not rely on hearing children to interpret for deaf parents. It takes away the innocence of childhood, and moreover, it takes away the privacy of adulthood."

In the past, the use of such people for communication purposes, while inappropriate, was common practice, and was not discouraged by any legislation. With the advent of the Disability Discrimination Act (1995), however, this is no longer necessarily the case.

The first sections of the Act, which relate to the provision of goods and services, and employment, have made it unlawful for service providers to refuse to provide a service to a disabled person, to provide that service to a lower standard, or to make it unreasonably difficult for a disabled person to avail themselves of that service (Section III).

It could clearly be argued that using a family member, rather than an appropriately qualified interpreter in settings such as those described above, might be seen to contradict this section of the act. In October 1999, another section of the act was implemented which deals with the provision of auxiliary aids or services (DDA, Section III, Par 21-4a–b). This section refers specifically to the provision of sign language interpreters, if they are required by Deaf people, and adds even more weight to the argument that inappropriate or untrained interpreters should not be used.

Communication is a two way process, and it might be suggested that midwives who continue to use family members as interpreters may be as much in danger of misunderstanding the women, and fail to identify risk factors, just as the Deaf woman may miss out on both the support and encouragement of the midwife during labour and even basic information on how to care for herself and her baby.

There are properly trained, bi-lingual interpreters who function as professionals, adhering to a strict Code of Ethics and confidentiality (Council for the Advancement of Communication with Deaf People, 1998), preserving the patient's confidentiality and the professional's integrity (something which would be in the best interest of both the patient and the practitioner). The use of a properly trained interpreter is also important to ensure quality of service. If anything were to happen, as a result of misinterpretation—especially in this case where the person acting as interpreter is not an adult—then there might well be grounds for an action for negligence.

Case Study

As has been mentioned already, there are a number of reasons why it may not be safe or acceptable for professionals to communicate with their Deaf clients using children or other family members as interpreters. An additional reason which was not highlighted above, but which is known to have happened on a number of occasions, is the deliberate misinterpretation of a message by the child in order to bring about the outcome most favoured by themselves.

The following is a simple example of this type of occurrence, and while it is not itself an actual account of real events, it is based upon events reported first hand to the authors.

Mrs Smith is a young Deaf mother. She already has two children, an 8-year-old daughter and a 3-year-old son. She is expecting another child, and is attending her local hospital for an ultrasound scan. Her 8-year-old daughter is with her, acting as her interpreter.

During the scan she is asked whether or not she wishes to know the sex of her baby. She does not, but her daughter, who is desperate to have a little sister, wants to know. Although Mrs Smith tells her daughter that she does not want to be told, the daughter translates her mother's response as 'yes please'. The information is duly given, and the child, now in possession of information which her mother did not want, is left to decide whether to pass this information on, or keep it to herself.

There are a number of issues raised by this scenario, and while it could be said that, at a first glance, no lasting harm has been done, there are quite serious implications here for the mother, in terms of her right to confidentiality, as well as a potential for internal difficulties to arise within the family. Furthermore, if this relatively undamaging scenario can occur, then there are situations in which the actions of a child, looking after his or her own interests, rather than those of the person for whom he or she is interpreting, could be much more serious, if not life threatening.

Implications for the Future

While there seems little doubt that midwifery, in common with other health services, has not always given the attention to detail necessary to ensure that Deaf women receive appropriate and accessible care, the new legislative structures and statutes will, in many cases, force the issue. This will probably mean that health professionals and their employing NHS trusts will insist upon the presence of qualified interpreters, in order to protect themselves from complaints and litigation.

There are, however, two ways in which sign language interpreters may be employed. They may, as is currently the norm, be freelance interpreters who then charge the trust for their services. Alternatively, they may be employees of the trust, whose services are then available to the health professionals within that trust as needed.

The former system may provide greater choice and continuity of care to the Deaf woman (who may use the same small pool of interpreters in a variety of situations over several years). This may include the woman having choice and control over the gender of her interpreter during delivery. The latter may be seen as giving greater control, including quality control on interpreters' qualifications, to the trusts.

Midwives are also very aware of the unpredictability, both of the exact time of onset and the length of labour, and unsocial hours at which this can occur. Callouts at unsociable hours are a feature of freelance interpreting. Midwives may already have experience of how well interpreting services for minority spoken languages work when provided by in-house services.

Conclusion

Although midwives may not meet many Deaf women in the course of their practice, it is essential that when they do, they protect both the woman and themselves by using appropriate professional interpreters. Midwives may also wish to contribute to the development of appropriate policies for their service, including considering ways in which the quality and autonomy of interpreting services can best be ensured, in order to protect deaf women's autonomy.

Notes

1. Our thanks to Norma Fryer and Fiona Dykes for their comments on drafts of this paper.

References

Bramwell, R., Harrington, F.J. and Harris, J. (2000) Deafness—disability or linguistic minority? In *British Journal of Midwifery* 8/4:222–224.
Commission of Enquiry into Human Aids to Communication (1992) *Communication is Your Responsibility.* John Knight Publicity, London.

Council for the Advancement of Communication with Deaf People (1998) *Code of Ethics* for Sign Language Interpreters, in *Directory 1998/99*, CACDP, Durham 2, 6–8.

Expert Maternity Group (1993) *Changing Childbirth*. HMSO London.

HMSO (1995) *Disability Discrimination Act 1995*, Chapter 50. HMSO, London.

NHS (1995) *The Patients Charter* Department of Health, London.

Harrington, F.J. (1998) Enabling Service Providers to meet the needs of Deaf clients *British Journal of Therapy and Rehabilitation*, 5/8.

Padden, C. (1980) The Deaf Community and the Culture of Deaf People. In C. Baker and R. Battison (eds) *Sign Language and the Deaf Community: Essays in honour of William C. Stokoe*. Silver Spring MD: National Association of the Deaf. 89–104.

Shackle, M. (1994) 'Mothers' pride and others' prejudice; a survey of disabled mothers' experiences of maternity'. The Maternity Alliance, London.

Thomas, C. and Curtis, P. (1997) 'Having a baby: some disabled women's reproductive experiences' Midwifery 13, 202–209.

Woodward, J. (1972) Implications for sociolinguistic research among the deaf. *Sign Language Studies*, 1:1–7.

U.K.C.C. (1996) *Midwives Rules and Code of Practice*. UKCC, London.

Interpreting in Social Services: setting the boundaries of good practice?
Frank J. Harrington

Introduction

Although the Social Services Department in England and Wales has only existed in its present form since the early 1970s, policy governing its statutory responsibility to provide services to certain groups of people who are considered to be vulnerable or at risk, including deaf people, can be traced back over a period of more than 50 years.

The initial statement which defined who was eligible to receive such services came in the National Assistance Act (HMSO 1948). It stated that "a Local Authority shall have the power to make arrangements for promoting the welfare of persons… who are blind, deaf or dumb, and other persons who are substantially and permanently handicapped by illness, injury or congenital deformity, or such other disabilities as may be prescribed by the minister" (HMSO 1948, Part III, Section 29 paragraph 1). Furthermore, the act states that the Local Authority had a clear duty to exercise these powers—in other words, such provision was not optional.

Those "suffering from a mental disorder" were added to this list of permanently disabled people in the Mental Health Act (HMSO 1959), and the act ensured that welfare professionals were identified as being responsible for ensuring that all of these groups of people received a service.

At various times, successive governments have re-defined the services which should be provided, and those eligible to receive such services, in legislative documents such as Chronically Sick and Disabled Persons Act (HMSO 1970) the Local Government Act (HMSO 1972),the Housing Acts (HMSO 1974 and 1980), Disabled Persons (Services, Consultation and Representation) Act (HMSO 1986), the National Health Service and Community Care Act (HMSO 1990) and the Disability Discrimination Act (HMSO 1995b).

Adapted from a paper given at INI, the first *Issues in Interpreting* conference. Durham University, 16 April 1994.

Section 195 of the Local Government Act, in its amendments to section 29 of the National Assistance Act, stated that 'The Secretary of State attaches importance to the development of specialist services to meet the particular need of any group of persons where this will most effectively meet those needs'. Further to this, the Disabled Persons (Services, Consultation and Rehabilitation) Act stated that in a situation where oral or written communication with a client is not possible as a result of their disability 'the local authority shall provide such services as, in their opinion, are necessary to ensure that any such incapacity does not:

1 prevent the authority from discharging their functions under this section in relation to the disabled person;
or
2 prevent the making of representations under this section by or on behalf of that person. (HMSO 1986, Chapter 3, part 1, sections 3–6)

Most recently, the Disability Discrimination Act has extended the responsibility for accessible service provision beyond the Social Services department and other statutory bodies, to a wide range of businesses and organisations (HMSO 1995b, Chapter 50, Section 1). Before the introduction of the first sections of the Disability Discrimination Act in December 1996, the Social Services department was not compelled to provide an interpreting service to its deaf clients, but it has always been recognised that, in order to receive a request for a service, or to be able to provide such a service to anyone fulfilling the criteria set out in these policies, the department had to be able to communicate appropriately with the person concerned.

In light of the above, it is clear that the Social Services Department has a responsibility to provide an appropriate service in an appropriate language to fully meet the needs of any of its clients, who, as a result of their deafness, are unable to communicate satisfactorily by means of either written or spoken English.

Social workers and relatives as interpreters

Historically, communication support services were provided to the deaf community by welfare officers, missionaries, social workers with deaf people or hearing children of deaf adults. There was no insistence that these people have specialist interpreting qualifications, although those who had trained as welfare officers for the deaf, through the Deaf Welfare Examination Board (DWEB), and prior to the establishment of the CACDP Register of Interpreters in 1981, held certificates which identified interpreting as part of their remit (Simpson 1990).

In spite of recent changes in social policy described above, little has been done to define or enforce minimum standards of skill and qualification required by those who provide interpreting services under these policies, and many interpreted events which take place in social and professional settings are still carried out using the services of untrained or non-specialist interpreters. In particular, the DDA does not stipulate the level or quality of service that must be provided, only that the provision must be 'reasonable' (HMSO 1995b, Part 1, section 19). The Disability Rights Commission will have an opportunity to do so in future, but whether or not this will happen is not known at this time.

Anecdotal evidence suggests that, in the past, it was often the case that professionals would rather use someone who could sign to interpret for them in an appointment, no matter how inappropriate or unskilled that person might have been, than cancel or postpone the appointment in the absence of a suitably qualified interpreter. This is still the case on occasion, and this general lack of awareness on the part of such professionals as to the appropriate qualification or skill levels of interpreters has also added to the difficulties already discussed.

There continue, then, to be a significant number of instances where untrained interpreters are facilitating communication between deaf people and a variety of hearing professionals. Exceptions to this, where policy developments have been made to try to ensure the use of appropriately trained and qualified interpreters, can be found primarily in the criminal justice system. The Police and Criminal Evidence Act codes of practice (HMSO 1995a) allow for deaf people to be interviewed only with the presence of a suitably qualified interpreter. In addition, it is expected that, as of December 2001, the Lord Chancellor's office will implement a policy prohibiting all except Registered Qualified Interpreters from working in courts, but similar policies are not expected to be developed in other public services and statutory authorities in the near future. The result of this is that the use of untrained or inappropriate interpreters is likely to continue in a variety of settings for as long as there is a dearth of appropriately trained and qualified people to provide interpreting services.

It might be argued that deaf people will want to exercise their right to choose who will communicate for them, or that the provision of someone, be they a signing social worker or a relative of the deaf person, is better than no-one at all. Maybe we shouldn't deny deaf people the right to choose, but, in a world where professionals are increasingly under threat of legal action when things go wrong, I believe that we do have a responsibility to demonstrate, to both deaf and hearing users of interpreting services, that higher standards of service and levels of 'safety' can only be achieved by improving the skills of interpreters through training, qualification and regulation (Turner 1996, Harrington 1997).

Relatives as untrained interpreters

It is almost impossible for relatives acting as interpreters to remain impartial in such situations. They may be asked to interpret for a doctor who is telling the deaf person that they have incurable cancer; they may be interpreting for a deaf person who is being told their mortgage arrears are such that they are about to be evicted. There are so many situations where impartiality is essential, and to expect this of people who are emotionally involved in the situation, especially if those people are children, is not acceptable.

Relatives acting as interpreters are not bound by any code of practice or ethical principles, and are not, therefore, bound to honour the confidentiality of those for whom they interpret. This clearly has its own implications within a local deaf community.

Finally, it may be possible that such a use of children is actually an abuse of their rights as children. Certainly, since the introduction of the Children's Act 1989, abuse of children is no longer seen only in the form of sexual and physical abuse or neglect, but also in terms of emotional abuse. Many people might feel that the term 'abuse' is a little strong. After all, most children who interpret do so willingly in order to help their parents, and often neither parents or children see anything wrong in what they do. The dangers are perhaps best summed up as follows:

We should not rely on hearing children to interpret for deaf parents. It takes away the innocence of childhood, and moreover, it takes away the privacy of adulthood. (John Bowis MP, former Under-Secretary of State for Health).

Mr Bowis' comments were made at a public meeting held in London in June 1993, which was held to discuss the implications for the Health Authority of the report *Communication is your Responsibility*, commissioned by the Panel of Four and published in 1992.

Social Workers as untrained interpreters

In the past, Social Workers were expected to provide an interpreting role, simply because there was no alternative (Scott Gibson 1990, Darby and Gregory 1995). It is now recognised, however, that interpreting is a distinct profession, and that independent, confidential interpreters exist so that social workers no longer need to undertake this work. There are, however, still a number of Social Services Departments in this country that fulfil their obligations to the deaf community by asking social workers to continue interpreting as part of their role. Equally, there are many social workers who are happy to continue to provide interpreting services as part of their job (Coutts 1994, Pickard 1993).

In a survey published in 1993 by ADSUP and the BDA, 42% of social workers with deaf people accepted that interpreting was still part of their job description, and 27% felt that interpreting should be seen as part of their role. In the same survey, 47% of Social Services Departments and 41% of Social Services managers, identified interpreting as an integral part of the social work role. Most interestingly, 74% of deaf people said that they expected to be able to receive an interpreting service of some kind from their social worker (Scott Gibson 1993). So, why might it be inappropriate for a social worker to undertake an interpreting role?

Society has a very specific notion of Social Services and their role in this country, and it is believed by many that whenever there is a social worker involved with a family, it is because they have some kind of problem. It may not be a justified sentiment, but for many people the very idea that they may need help from the Department gives them a feeling of inadequacy. They lose their self esteem and value, and in their own eyes they become second best.

A social work colleague of mine once told me that, in his opinion, it is not because of any specific disability, real or perceived, that disabled or deaf people need the support of social workers. The only people who really need social workers are those who, in spite of any disability they may or may not have, are simply incapable of coping with life.

Whether or not you agree with this sentiment, it is true that there are many hundreds of deaf people in this country whose only need is for an interpreter. They have no problems coping with life. As long as there is an appropriate person available to support them in their communication needs, and they have access to the equipment they need, such as text-phones and loop systems, in order to live full and independent lives, they will probably never need access to the other services offered by the Department.

Yet, if a deaf person has no choice but to approach the Social Services Department in order to receive communication support from a social worker, he or she would most likely become a client of that worker and of the Department, and it has been argued for a number of years that this is not appropriate for someone whose only need is communication support.

The interpreters' Code of Practice (section 4) expects interpreters to maintain a level of confidentiality regarding the private matters of individual deaf people for whom they interpret (CACDP 2000). While the Social Services Department has its own notion of confidentiality, open cases can be discussed between a number of workers in the same department, and any social worker can, if necessary, have access to client files at any time.

This is not to say that interpreters do not keep a record of some of their assignments. It is a sad fact that, in this day and age, even interpreters have to safeguard themselves, and anyone interpreting for the police, or in a court might be well advised to keep a record of certain assignments, in case their skills are called into question at some future date. Neither is it the case that social workers are unaware of the issues raised by their acting as interpreters. They may go to great lengths to separate out the information about their clients that they know from each of their separate roles, but this is a difficult and unnecessary task for them to have to do. No matter how hard they try, however, there must be a danger that their social work decisions may be influenced by information to which they should not and would not have been party if an independent interpreter had been used.

The BASW Code of Ethics, published in 1985, stated quite clearly that it is the responsibility of the social worker to ensure that his/her client's '… dignity, individuality, rights and responsibility will be safeguarded' (principle no.2) In contrast to this the interpreters' Code of Practice makes it clear that interpreters are not expected to give advice or offer personal opinions (Section 7). Again there is a clear potential for conflict of interest here.

To give another example, the CACDP Code of Practice is clear on the notion of impartiality (Section 5). Yet the BASW Code of Ethics states that the social worker '… will help his/her clients increase the range of choices open to them and their powers to make decisions…' (Principle no. 4). Anyone acting both as interpreter and social worker would find it difficult to adhere to both of these principles at the same time.

There has long been a need for a distinction to be made between these two professions, and this was clearly voiced by the Alliance of Deaf Service Users and Providers (ADSUP) in the report on the Consultation on Human Aids to Communication.

> This organisation believes that social work and interpreting are two distinct professions, each having its own training, Code of Ethics and principles of practice… It is inappropriate for one person to be carrying out the roles of social workers and interpreters in the same situation. Similarly it is inappropriate for the duties of interpreting and social work to be combined in one post. (Panel of Four 1992:31)

Interpreters as employees of the Social Services Department

One way in which Social Services Departments have got around the problem of separating out the Social Work and Interpreter roles has been to employ 'in house' interpreters. In a survey carried out as part of the Council for the Advancement of Communication with Deaf people (CACDP) report *Agents for Change* (Harrington 1994) it was found that there were 16 Social Services Departments in England and Wales identified as employing either a full time or part time Sign Language Interpreter.

At that time, only one of the 16 interpreters was a fully qualified member of the CACDP Register, 14 were stage III holders and were registered with CACDP as trainee interpreters, and the other was a Stage II holder. While this situation has changed somewhat in recent years, due to moves within the profession to raise the standard of interpreting services, recently publicised job advertisements indicate that a majority of interpreters employed by Social Services Departments are trainees rather than members of the Register.

It may be argued that a Social Services Department is not an appropriate place for an interpreting service to be based, and certainly, given some of the reasons suggested above as to why social workers are not appropriate people to interpret, this argument may well be valid. There are certainly some dilemmas that are raised by this situation. Let me illustrate these by drawing on my own experience, as an interpreter based in a Social Services Department for almost four years.

When I first took up the post of social services interpreter, I was based in the local offices of the Social Services Department. Following a number of lengthy discussions, it was agreed that, for the sake of client confidentiality, I might be better located in a separate office in the local deaf centre, with my own telephone and administrative support. Although the social workers for deaf people were based in the same centre, deaf people were able to access the interpreting service without needing to go to the social work office.

Over a period of two years, the roles of social workers and the interpreter in this particular situation became quite clearly defined, and social workers became more aware of the distinctions between referrals for social work support, and those which were clearly requests for interpreting services. In situations where an interpreter was needed, but where the deaf person might also have needed advocacy or other support, both the interpreter and a social worker would attend the assignment in their separate roles.

Any notes of assignments, or service provision statistics that the interpreter kept, or was asked to make available to the Department, were kept anonymously, and neither names, dates nor any other details of interpreting assignments were available in files or other documents to which the social work team had access.

In my particular situation this system worked well, although achieving it was both difficult and time consuming. It demanded a lot of discussion and compromise to ensure that the service being provided was acceptable as well as accessible to both the social services department and the deaf service users, and there were a number of problems to be overcome.

As long as a social services department employing an interpreter is open to the notion that their interpreter can maintain a degree of autonomy, then the sense in which deaf people feel compromised by the situation can be minimised. However, the very fact that the interpreting service is based in the Social Services Department can itself be a deterrent to many deaf people who might otherwise make use of an interpreting service.

Providing interpreting services through external agencies

The main alternative for most service providers, Social Services departments included, to employing a full time interpreter, is for them to fund or part-fund an interpreting service or Communication Support Unit (CSU). In the past, Social Services departments found this a difficult notion to entertain, primarily because it was costly, and because, traditionally, interpreting services were provided by social workers. However, the introduction of the National Health Service and Community Care Act in 1992, followed by the Disability Discrimination Act in 1995, has enabled this practice to become increasingly common.

The CCA brought about changes that made Social Services departments responsible for purchasing appropriate services for their clients from a variety of sources, rather than simply providing them from existing internal resources. While a number of the departments that employed their own interpreters continued to do so, others were persuaded to fund or part-fund regional interpreting services. The increase in awareness of deaf issues and the responsibility of service providers to make their services accessible, brought about through the

120 DDA, has also contributed to the steady increase in the numbers of independent interpreting agencies around the country.

It is to be hoped that the work, and recommendations, of the new Disability Rights Commission will further enhance the provision of quality services to disabled people, and in particular, the provision of quality interpreting services for deaf people. Since the introduction of the DDA, the expectation that 'reasonable provision' will suffice has meant that many services have, in reality, been somewhat inadequate. By defining more clearly the minimum requirements of a service or provision for it to be deemed reasonable, the commission could have a real impact on the future enforcement of the DDA, and on the level of equality afforded to deaf and disabled people. Whether or not this will happen, only time will tell.

Conclusion

In spite of the increasing numbers of interpreting agencies, and the raising of standards in interpreting, that have been seen in the last decade, there is still a real need to further clarify the roles and responsibilities of those involved in the provision of statutory services, in particular in relation to the provision of interpreting services for deaf people.

It is clear that Social Services departments have a need, and a responsibility, to provide interpreting services to their deaf clients, and this paper has suggested that it is not appropriate for these services to be provided by 'ad hoc' interpreters. Furthermore, it is becoming increasingly unacceptable for social workers to carry out interpreting tasks. If properly organised, and carefully managed, it may be that Social Services departments could provide appropriate 'in house' interpreting services to meet the needs of a local deaf community, but, ideally, provision of interpreting services should come from independent interpreting services, funded or purchased by the Social Services department. Certainly there is some way to go, both in terms of policy development (with the continuing changes to the Disability Discrimination Act, and the advent of a Disability Rights Commission) and in terms of public and organisational awareness, if Social Services departments are to provide consistent and high quality interpreting services to their deaf clients.

References

BASW (1985) *Codes of Practice for Social Workers*.
CACDP (2000) *Directory*. CACDP: Durham. 1.7–1.10.
Coutts, K (1994) The Social Worker's Role. *Deafness* 10/1.
Darby A. and Gregory, S. (1995) Training Social Workers with Deaf people: the story of a course. *Deafness* 11/1.
Harrington F.J. (1994) Interpreters Employed by Social Services Departments. CACDP *Agents for Change*. CACDP: Durham.
—— (1998) Enabling Service providers to meet the needs of Deaf clients. *British Journal of Therapy and Rehabilitation*, 5/8.
HMSO (1948) *National Assistance Act*. HMSO: London.
—— (1959) *Mental Health Act*. HMSO: London.
—— (1970) *Chronically Sick and Disabled Persons Act*. HMSO: London.
—— (1972) *Local Government Act*. HMSO: London.
—— (1974) *Housing Act*. HMSO: London.
—— (1980) *Housing Act*. HMSO: London.
—— (1984) *Police and Criminal Evidence Act*, Chapter 60. HMSO: London.
—— (1986) *Disabled Persons (Services, Consultation and Representation) Act*. HMSO: London.
—— (1990) *National Health Service and Community Care Act*. HMSO: London.
—— (1995a) *Police and Criminal Evidence Act codes of Practice (3)*. HMSO: London.
—— (1995b) *Disability Discrimination Act*, Chapter 50. HMSO: London.
Panel of Four (1992) *Communication is Your Responsibility: The Commission of Enquiry into Human Aids to Communication*. John Knight: England.
Pickard, N. (1993) Sign Language interpreting—relationship with social services, social workers and community care. *Deafness*, 9/2.
Scott Gibson, L. (1993) *Social workers with deaf people and interpreting: a survey*. Carlisle: BDA.
—— (1990) Sign Language Interpreting, an Emerging Profession. Gregory and Hartley (eds) (1991) *Constructing Deafness*. Open University: Milton Keynes. 253–258.
Simpson, T.S. (1990) A Stimulus to Learning, a Measure of Ability.

Gregory and Hartley (eds) (1991) *Constructing Deafness.* Open University: Milton Keynes. 217–225.

Turner, G.H. (1996) Regulation and Responsibility: The relationships between Deaf people and interpreters. *Deaf Worlds* 12/1.

4
ANALYSES OF INTERPRETING PRACTICES
Law

The bilingual, bimodal courtroom: a first glance
Graham H. Turner

Introduction

In this initial exploratory paper,[1] I aim to take a closer look at features of interaction between signing and speaking people mediated by a BSL/English interpreter. The spotlight will be on interaction in an area that many interpreters refuse to touch because of its inherent complexity, i.e. the courtroom. The paper can be seen, rather than as a detailed analysis of the scenario in question, as initial broad-brushed background material identifying certain issues to be considered in the course of more detailed analysis.[2]

In the longer term, such study should not only provide valuable information to feed back into training and awareness programmes, but also offer insights into what goes on in the course of bilingual, bimodal (that is, signed and spoken) talk-in-interaction. To borrow a phrase from Deborah Cameron's keynote paper (Cameron 1994) to the British Association for Applied Linguistics conference, it's a case of "putting practice into theory": analysing practices as a potentially fruitful way of grounding and developing theory.

The tension that is felt within applied linguistic circles between 'doing theories' and 'doing practices' comes into very sharp focus throughout sign linguistics, and it is always worth trying to keep in mind what language researchers are aiming to achieve in this context. In keeping with the valuable critique of research practices that is set out in Cameron et al (1992), an 'empowering' approach to this study has been adopted wherever possible. The study is, for instance, informed to a considerable degree by practitioners' own beliefs about their interpreting practices.[3]

Patsy Lightbown's opening plenary at the recent American Association for Applied Linguistics annual meeting (Lightbown 1994) counseled that we must (a) continue to admit what we do not know and (b) refrain from making premature pronouncements. Sign linguistics is a young field, but the applied issues are—after many decades of oppression of signed languages—urgently in need of attention. As a consequence, we frequently find ourselves torn between two goals. On the one hand, as scientists, we want to assert our right (and indeed our duty) to be ignorant and naïve and to explore questions to which we do not yet know the answers. On the other—knowing the positive effect linguists' work can have in terms of empowering signing communities—we want to fulfil our role as agents for change by the application of what little we know. Within the sign linguistics field, this position, and the stance of engagement-beyond-the-theoretical which this paper implicitly adopts, has been most clearly articulated by Mary Brennan (1986:14-16).

Firstly, then, I shall try to put my remarks into some kind of context, and then go on to indicate some dimensions or themes that seem worthy of attention.

Context

Why is the courtroom a particularly important area to study in the UK? After all, article six of the European Convention on Human Rights already includes the instruction that criminal suspects have the right to be informed in a language which they understand about any accusation made against them, and also to have free assistance of an interpreter in court. A December 1993 judgement of the European Court of Human Rights—the Kamasinski case of a US citizen imprisoned in Austria—also stressed that the institution responsible for providing the interpreter is subsequently responsible for the standard and competence of the actual service (Polack and Corsellis 1990).

Is there any reason to be concerned about that standard? The general legal interpreting field in the UK has come under some scrutiny lately—notably through the work of the Nuffield Interpreter Project (Nuffield Interpreter Project 1993)—and a number of cases have been quite well publicised. In 1981, for example, a woman who had come from rural Pakistan to an arranged marriage in Birmingham, England went to prison having killed her husband with an iron bar. She pleaded guilty and served four years of a life sentence before the Court of Appeal acknowledged that the interpreter—an accountant—had spoken to her in Urdu, while her preferred language was in fact Punjabi and she spoke very little Urdu. She probably grasped virtually nothing of what was going on, and certainly not the distinction between murder and manslaughter crucial to her life sentence (Parker 1993).

In a case involving BSL/English interpreting some years ago, a Deaf man was expected to stand trial for rape with interpretation provided by the holder of a Stage 1 certificate in BSL skills—a language skills certificate, not an interpreting qualification. It is required by the regulatory body (the Council for the Advancement of Communication with Deaf People) that a Stage 1 course involve 60 hours of teaching (CACDP no date:2). The exam takes approximately 15 minutes. In fact, the situation with respect to BSL/English interpreting is in many respects markedly better than for most linguistic minorities in the UK (Nuffield Interpreter Project 1993). There are official registers of signing interpreters, and police forces keep their own lists for police station work.

One source of pressure that impacts upon this type of situation is from the interpreters themselves, who are struggling towards notions of increased professionalisation (see Scott Gibson 1990, 1994). "Call me mercenary," wrote then-trainee interpreter Mohammad Islam in a recent issue of the Association for Sign Language Interpreters magazine (Islam 1993:31):

> "but I am not getting up at two in the morning, driving for an hour to the police station, working for two hours, spending another hour driving home—all for £26. Would you?"

An impossible situation

One conclusion that might be drawn from all this is that there is a fundamental problem in a judicial process that requires interpreting. The system is full of holes which can add spin in any direction. In fact, there are those—such as the Canadian Freedom of Choice Movement—who have concluded (Berk-Seligson 1990:215) that the presence of an interpreter is actively prejudicial to the interests of the minority-language-using defendant. The group has argued that the defendant has a right to a trial conducted entirely in his or her preferred language. The Supreme Court of Canada has disagreed.

If interpreters must be used, then perhaps it is most advantageous to consider this a tactical strategy, just another part of the legal 'contest'. This kind of perspective has been quite convincingly articulated by the Australian Kathy Laster (1990:17):

"The law, while formally assigning only a narrow role to interpreters, in practice makes ambiguous and contradictory demands of them. As a result, non-English speakers are not necessarily always better off when an interpreter is used. The issue whether to use an interpreter in individual cases therefore is best conceived of as a tactical one rather than as an abstract question of 'rights'. The advantage of this approach is that it focuses attention on the aspects of the legal system itself which militate against social justice for non-English speakers rather than allowing interpreters to be regarded as 'the problem' requiring 'reform'."

This proposal clearly requires greater attention, since the implications are considerable. As Ruth Morris concludes from her case study of the Ivan Demjanjuk trial, it seems minimally to be the case that interpretation of legal proceedings has "a persona of its own" (1989a:36).

Perceptions

What are the sources of the problems in legal interpreting? It seems that one set of problems derives from various participants' perceptions of norms and practices relating to this setting.

There are general perceptions to do with Deaf people[4] and signed languages that are as likely to be held by legal professionals as by other members of the public. Deaf communities all over the world are still struggling to escape the oppressive weight of pathological or medical models of what it means to be Deaf, in favour of cultural and linguistic models (see Lane 1992, Padden and Humphries 1988). Non-Deaf participants in the court are as likely as non-Deaf people in any other walk of life to expect someone else to be speaking 'on behalf of' the Deaf person—the 'does he take sugar?' syndrome. This can result in a great deal of confusion over the role of the interpreter. Many people doubt the interpreter's impartiality, or indeed assume partiality. The result (as reported by a number of practitioners) is that interpreters are frequently instructed by the court to 'just relay everything verbatim'. Such an instruction serves only to underline (a) the court's lack of awareness of, or trust in, interpreting procedures, and (b) a lack of appreciation of what must occur in the very nature of the process of interpreting.

The visual-gestural nature of BSL also raises problems of perception of at least three kinds. Firstly, many other participants in the process may have the sneaking feeling that they understand, perhaps quite clearly, what's being signed. Lochrie (no date) gives an example from a situation involving a late colleague of his:

> "The Advocate asked the deaf witness … 'Are you single?', the interpreter changed the question to 'Are you married?' which signs easier. The witness shook his head vigorously. The interpreter speaks and says 'Yes, I am single'. The Advocate is nonplussed and says 'But the witness shook his head'. The interpreter then explained that the words are you single would not be easy for the witness to understand, so I asked him 'Are you married?'. The Judge, while understanding the situation, cautioned the interpreter."

Secondly, there is an issue of awareness concerning perceptions of the adequacy of court records. Court records—and records in police stations, where audio recording is standard practice—are kept as written English text, with no further checks and balances built into the system for being assured of interpreting accuracy. BSL does not have a conventional writing system comparable to that for English.[5] Keeping a written record of the signing itself would be impracticable under current constraints.

Thirdly, it is widely believed that signed languages are modelled on and run structurally parallel to the spoken languages with which they co-exist (though attempts have been made to create artificial systems organised along these lines, or to adapt natural signed languages to accommodate spoken/written linguistic structural principles—see Anthony 1971, Bergman 1979, Bornstein et al 1975, Gustason et al 1975). It is therefore widely, and entirely erroneously, believed that the interpreter's job is therefore a simple matter of adjusting the modality from speech to sign and back.

BSL/English interpreters are no different from any others in many respects, though, such as the outsider's perception that their task is a straightforward matter of input and output, a simple 'conduit' task. Many lawyers, judges and other legal professionals indicate (Butler and Noaks 1992) that they are not in the least concerned with the need for competent interpretation, assuming instead that interpretation is an entirely mechanical task requiring negligible analytical skills. That lack of concern is itself part of the problem, because (a) it means that any time the interpreter becomes obtrusive for any reason, that will automatically be viewed as something going wrong; and (b) because it is indicative of the fact that, as long as the interpreter is producing something that looks and especially sounds plausible, there is nothing to worry about. I shall come back to this point.

What about the interpreter's own perception of his/her role? Here, too, there is potential for conflict. It is not unusual for the interpreter to be expected to be, and thus to get drawn into being, an agent of the court. One result of this is the interpreter finding him/herself taking on the interactional patterns of the court instead of merely facilitating their flow. Susan Berk-Seligson (1990:62) provides a clear example of this in the Spanish-English courtroom in the USA. A long exchange is reproduced in which the judge and attorney are trying to get the defendant to state her plea, guilty or not guilty. The defendant keeps answering 'yes' (meaning 'guilty'). Finally, the attorney tells the interpreter "So she's gotta say it, tell her to say it", and the interpreter takes on an instructing role, herself saying (in Spanish), "That is, you have to say it. Say it! What are you?" Anecdotal reports tell us that such exchanges are not uncommon in the BSL/English courtroom.

Conversely, consider this (Nusser 1993:4), especially point three:

"The facts are clear:
1   Though Americans believe that all people should be treated equally, hearing people have more power (i.e. employment and educational opportunities, role models, language recognition, status, etc).
2   In a mixed group of individuals, such as in an interpreting assignment or professional conference, relational power dynam-

ics also exist because of differing values and stereotypes.
3   Hearing interpreters must try as much as possible to act as allies among members of a linguistic and cultural minority."

It is absolutely true that BSL/English interpreters are trained to know about Deaf people's lives and Deaf community and cultural issues. Models of interpreting are changing (McIntire and Sanderson in press, Roy 1993a, Witter-Merithew 1986). But I think one can clearly see where this statement might be perceived to lead—in respect of its effect on the neutrality, or otherwise, of the interpretation—if followed through in a courtroom situation. Other professionals in the courtroom can feel threatened by interaction taking place in a language which they do not understand. 'Interpreter as ally' is a position which must be treated, especially in public fora, with the greatest of care, and will doubtless be a point of considerable debate in the near future.

The interpreter also knows that it is part and parcel of his/her role to be a cultural broker or mediator, smoothing over gaps in cultural knowledge. Learning to do that effectively is part of the training. But again there seem to be lines to be drawn. The point is very well made by Jon Leeth, one of Berk-Seligson's interviewees (Berk-Seligson 1990:40), who said:

> "The Court Interpreter's Act is not designed as an intercultural tool to integrate people into American society. It is an Act designed to bring justice to these individuals just as if they were English speaking. It is not designed to give them an advantage...only to prevent miscarriages of justice. They have the same responsibilities as anybody else...to say 'I don't know what you're talking about. Could you make that clear?'"

One BSL/English interpreter I interviewed recently made a similar point. This person said:

> "I interpreted a case once where the judge and the clerk went into a heated exchange on some technical detail. As I tried to convey something of it to the Deaf defendant, his counsel said to me, 'Don't bother! It's too technical. He won't understand it'. To which I replied, 'That's okay: he has a right not to understand'."

Some features of Court talk

If there are problems for interpreters of a linguistic nature, where are they? There is—as there has long been in the wider sphere (e.g. Crystal and Davy 1969)—a strong feeling that the particular vocabulary used in the courtrooms is the real problem (Caccamise et al 1991; in the UK, the point is also implicit in the recent Royal Commission's recommendation (HMSO 1993) that glossaries of technical terms be developed for minority languages). And even those whose first language is English would acknowledge that the specialised and somewhat arcane formal language of the court can, in itself, cause major problems of comprehension.

Powerless speech

The lexical problems are certainly an issue, but there are others, more disturbing for the fact that they are not widely appreciated. A whole host of issues are raised in connection with work done by William O'Barr and associates (O'Barr 1982), demonstrating that the features of what has been dubbed 'powerless speech' can play a significant role in courtrooms. Bear in mind that, in court, participants seek to appear honest, trustworthy, and so on, and that judges and juries use these impressions in framing their decisions. Powerless speech is associated—in the court setting—with weakness, indecision and evasiveness.

These features include, for example, the group of items known as hedges—'kind of', 'sort of', 'I guess', 'you know'—which sound non-committal, cautious, hesitant, uncertain or indecisive. Observation confirms that they are sometimes introduced into the simultaneous, unscripted language produced as BSL-to-English interpretation. Other features of powerless speech can also be heard being introduced as a kind of by-product of the interpreting circumstances.

These points are addressed with respect to the work of interpreters in considerable detail by Susan Berk-Seligson (1990:148ff). It is beyond the scope of the present paper to draw detailed parallels between Berk-Seligson's findings, relating to Spanish/English interpretation, and the situations under scrutiny here. One can, however, begin to see that one not unlikely effect of the interpreter's intervention between the overt conversational participants is that the contributions of the signing person are rendered more or less 'powerful' than the original texts. In other words, the impact of testimony given by a Deaf person in court can be altered for better or worse in the interpreted rendition. No analysis of 'powerless signing' has ever been done to date, and so it is impossible to say whether the reverse effect is also occurring.

Progress of discourse

The progress of the discourse is an additional matter for attention. O'Barr (1982:76-83) compares 'narrative style' as a discourse pattern in court—i.e. longer, more elaborately constructed sections of talk—against 'fragmented style', whereby the discourse is broken up into shorter turns, for instance in rapid question-and-answer exchanges. 'Narrative style' has the appearance of being credible and confident, and is encouraged by lawyers asking open-ended questions to their own witnesses: 'fragmented style' is almost inevitably the result of tightly constrained, quick-fire questioning. Thus, as Berk-Seligson makes abundantly clear (1990:178), if interpretation renders the message more or less fragmented than the original utterance, it has altered the effect of what was signed or said. Such alterations, though their effects may not be immediately apparent, are unlikely to be inconsequential, particularly when they accumulate throughout the duration of a section of testimony.

Of course, question-and-answer as a mode of exchange is very typical of courtroom interaction, and so it matters greatly that interpreters are aware and in control of the effect of how they present questions (cf. Eades 1988; 1992 for discussion of cultural differences in patterns of questioning and their effect on the non-interpreted courtroom). Brenda Danet (Danet 1980) has shown that questions vary in the extent to which they coerce or constrain the answer.

1   "You left the pub at midnight...."
    A declarative that does not ostensibly even ask a question, but leaves the witness to challenge if he/she wishes, is maximally constraining.
2   "Did you do it?" or "Did you leave at 7pm or 8pm?"
    Any kind of question that gives a limited number of choices is still clearly constraining: it is very difficult, for instance, to challenge the premiss upon which a question is founded when all the court is

interested in is 'just answer the question: yes or no?'.
3 "Where were you on the night of the twelfth?"
WH-questions like this are much more open, giving the respondent more scope to tell things their own way.
4 "Can you tell the court what happened?"
This kind of 'requestion' is typically used by lawyers to let their own witnesses tell the story comfortably, in their own words.

Danet shows that the more coercive the question, the greater the tendency for short, fragmented, powerless answers. Clearly, then, the interpreter's control of exactly how these questions can be interpreted is crucial.

Linguistic manipulation

The adversarial contest that the court engages in is also characterised by a degree of linguistic manipulation to control testimony. I will briefly mention two classic examples. The first shows that a skilled questioner can introduce presuppositions that constrain witnesses' answers—and which the interpreter must somehow faithfully maintain. In an experimental study, in which subjects were first shown a short film as evidence, Loftus and Zanni famously showed that the query "Did you see the broken headlight?" produced affirmative responses more frequently than "Did you see a broken headlight?" (Loftus and Zanni 1975). The second example (Loftus and Palmer 1974) showed that asking "About how fast were the two cars going when they smashed into each other?" produces higher speeds in answers than "About how fast were the two cars going when they hit each other?" These examples seem quite clearly to demonstrate the degree of absolute harmony the interpreter must achieve between source message and interpretation in order to be truly unobtrusive or non-distorting in the courtroom.

Linguistic image

I would like to mention one additional issue to do with linguistic image, i.e. the impression one gives simply through one's own vocal presentation. Matched guise testing—in which listeners are asked to rate various voice styles, without realising that they are actually hearing the same person using different 'guises'—has shown admirably that dynamic delivery, fast speech rate, lack of pauses and repetitions and 'normal', steady voice quality are all associated by hearers of English with notions of competence, trustworthiness and likeability (Berk-Seligson 1990:147). Simultaneous interpretation is not the best place in the world to look for examples of such vocal presentation: it is in the nature of the task—given the cognitive processing being done incessantly by the interpreter, for instance—that these qualities are going to be difficult to achieve.

Linguistic image also comes into play here in connection with our lack of knowledge about how different varieties of BSL are viewed and perceived by other users of the language. Are there signed accents associated with, for instance, boredom and lack of inspiration just as there are amongst spoken varieties? We do not know. On the other hand, we do know from accounts of hearers' attitudes to accents of English (see, for instance, Giles 1970; 1971) that the interpreter who happens to have a strong West Midlands accent may be giving out a potentially misleading and damaging impression of the Deaf person whose comments they are giving voice to.

Issues in Deaf Courts

In the following section, I will briefly identify some issues directly related to bimodal interpreting in legal settings. I use the term 'Deaf court' as a shorthand for 'court in which a Deaf person and an interpreter are active participants'.

Eyegaze

As Diana Eades has found in her very illuminating work in courts with speakers of Australian Aboriginal English (Eades 1988, 1992), averting your eyegaze from the court looks evasive. But it is in the nature of signed languages that Deaf people will do so. They will, for instance, be looking at the interpreter when the cross-examining barrister wants to look them in the eye at the point of the crucial question.

And it is in the nature of signed languages that Deaf people will, as far as the court is concerned, lose their eyegaze almost at random into the middle distance if they are ever given an opportunity to launch into any kind of complex narrative answer (the effect of role shifting and use of eyegaze to locate referents, et cetera).

Exchange norms

Anecdotal accounts from Deaf people suggest that question-and-answer is not a typical form of exchange within the Deaf community, and that longer, more narrative contributions are more common. The constraints of a courtroom system managed in such a manner may serve to disadvantage BSL users (cf. Eades 1988, 1992).

Secondly, because there will usually be one interpreter relaying messages in both directions during any one exchange, at any point where there is overlapping talk (i.e. two or more signed or spoken utterances being made simultaneously), the interpreter is forced to decide whose talk to represent (Roy 1993b). Because there may be two modalities being used at once by two participants, it is perfectly possible for speakers and signers to overlap each other for seconds at a time with no-one feeling uncomfortable—except the interpreter!

Slow interaction

There will always tend to be a moment between the end of the Deaf person's signed answer, and the start of the next spoken question during which only the interpreter talks. Since the interpreter's presence will introduce a time lag, it will be difficult to aggressively cross-examine the Deaf witness. Of course, no one is supposed to harrass the witness anyway, but attempts are nevertheless made to do so, and the interpreter's presence introduces a discrepancy between what happens otherwise and what happens in a Deaf court.

As Emmanuel Schegloff (Schegloff 1994), Adam Jaworski (Jaworski 1993) and others have been showing recently, silence plays no small part in everyday spoken interaction, and reactions occurring or not occurring (i.e. silences) at any point in the interaction are a significant element, contributing to the patterns of discourse. In response to a comment about how late one is for work (made in the hope that an offer of a lift might be forthcoming), for instance, a silence can be extremely eloquent. In a 'Deaf court', there are both unusual silences in the lagtime where the Deaf person signs and the interpreter has not yet begun to voice over; and there are 'delayed reactions' by both parties to each other's contributions (i.e. the reaction time is conditioned by the lagtime).

Politeness

Firstly, if, as Berk-Seligson demonstrates (Berk-Seligson 1990:154-169), politeness is a favourable strategy in court, then interpreters need to know a great deal more than is presently known (precious little) about politeness marking in BSL. Signed languages tend not to have direct person-to-person forms of address. Interaction typically does not begin until eyegaze is established: once it has been established, identifying the addressee by name is superfluous. So when the court is addressing the judge as 'Your Honour', what is the interpreter to do?

Secondly, one aspect of the impersonal nature of much legal interaction is the use of the full names of witnesses and other individuals named in testimony. In a recently observed trial, the interpreter reduced these forms to first name terms. "Did you see Arthur Jones enter the premises?" became "Did you see Arthur enter the premises?" The testimony has been altered, and native-user intuitions at least suggest that the latter utterance is considerably less formal and forbidding. Does this constitute cultural bridging—on the basis that Deaf people would not use full names—or a subtle but significant adjustment in the court procedures? Certainly this is a question of a type worthy of further attention.

Thirdly, I would like to mention here another phenomenon noted by Diana Eades (1992:8-10) that she refers to as 'gratuitous concurrence'—i.e. answering 'yes' or 'no' to questions without understanding them, just in order to get the business over with. This practice is encapsulated in a BSL sign which might be glossed as 'nod indiscriminately'. This sign relates to a practice widely commented on in Deaf-hearing relations—pretense of understanding of, or wilful disregard for, a message conveyed incomprehensibly, typically due to poor signing skills on the part of a hearing person attempting to communicate with Deaf people—and it seems very likely that it occurs in court as elsewhere.

Anticipating questions

It is appropriate in BSL interaction to use headshake and nod in anticipation of certain answers when asking questions: but the interpreter who does this without great care will be leaning into or presuggesting the expected answer. Other questions can become problematic due to the unaddressed assumption, even among interpreters, of word-to-word equivalence between BSL and English. Translating the English question "How did you feel about that?", in a sentence using the sign commonly glossed as 'how', to many BSL users actually means "By what process did you feel about that?"

Indirect questions

It is commonly reported by BSL/English interpreters that when they interpret English indirect questions—"They asked who was in the shop, and you explained, is that correct?"—into BSL, they are treated by default as if they were in fact direct questions of some sort. This can cause all sorts of problems in question-and-answer exchange: the response "Sally was in the shop: I've already told you this!" would be the kind of response an interpreter often finds him/herself giving voice to in such a situation.

Visual encoding

Many people manage, surprisingly frequently, to overlook the fact that signed languages encode meaning visually. Of course, fingerspelling exists, and many Deaf people are quite happy to see interpreters using fingerspelling when no conventional BSL sign is available to them (Sutton-Spence & Woll 1990, 1993). Many other Deaf people, however, are not sufficiently fluent in English to access meaning via fingerspelling in this way.

And BSL is fundamentally a visual language, a point that is made most clearly and followed through most profoundly by Mary Brennan (Brennan 1992). The result of this is that, for instance, in a recent murder trial, the interpreter needed to know how the murder was perpetrated—it was a stabbing—and to render the English word 'murder' with the sign that might be glossed as 'stab'.

BSL is a language that tends not to use umbrella terms like 'vehicle', 'weapon' or 'assault'. Any weapon one could mention in BSL has a lexical form that is consonant with its visual image: any form of assault likewise, and so on. It is impossible to give coherent visual form to the concept of 'weapon' as a category.

BSL is also a spatial language. So if English says "the two cars crashed", the form taken by the signed interpretation will be influenced by the spatial layout—whether the cars crashed head-on, side-on, et cetera. Interpreters are trained to become adept at using the spatial domain—as native signers do—to establish points of reference and to maintain these points throughout a chunk of discourse. In fact, of course, the interpreter, in attempting to process at incredible speed the information coming across to him/her will make what he/she hears or sees fit to his/her mental model of the scenario. This can cause problems. Observation of an interpreted trial dealing with a violent attack revealed a situation in which it was not until the third day of the trial that the interpreter realised they had consistently reversed the positions of the defendant and the victim. In this instance, it did not become significant, but one day it may.

It is a common strategy among interpreters to solve the problem of visual ambiguity in the English wording (which cannot be sustained in BSL) by offering a series of alternatives. So the interpretation of the English question "How did you get into the factory grounds?" might take the signed form more literally equivalent to "Did you get into the factory grounds by climbing over the wall, through a window, breaking in the door, or what?" The question (specifically in respect of the possible answers it foregrounds) has been altered in the interpretation.

Once again, lack of awareness on the part of the court as to the fundamentally visual nature of the language means that any time when the interpreter has to come out of his/her normatively non-participatory role in order to clarify on grounds such as those noted above, the court is reminded that the interpreter is there and is not a robot undertaking a mechanical task unaffected by the possibility of human error. The interpreter runs the risk of looking incompetent, but the real problem is others' lack of appreciation of differences in the nature of the languages being used.

Co-construction

One of the interactional issues that is beginning to come to the fore in work on this project is to do with the necessarily multi-party nature of interpreter-mediated interaction. A typical model of 'the best of all interpreted worlds' would have the interpreter utterly unobtrusive and the dialogue continuing as if it were monolingual. But since this is not the case, what are the implications of the interpreter's presence for this as talk-in-interaction in which there are, in fact, minimally three co-actors (Roy 1989, Wadensjö 1992)?

The concept of co-construction, or 'discourse as an interactional achievement', is currently enjoying attention from scholars such as Charles Goodwin (1994), Marjorie Harness Goodwin (1994) and Emmanuel Schegloff (1994) as a central process in social life. Co-construction is conceived as a joining together of participants in the joint production and interpretation of utterances, ideas, and so on. One of the central implications of the idea is that meaning in talk is necessarily not something one person does by themself: meaning is created between producers and perceivers, speakers and hearers. In the interpreted situation, therefore, meanings are in a sense developed and distributed between producer, conveyor and perceiver. What happens if we look into the bilingual, bimodal courtroom for evidence of co-construction?

Well, first of all, there are instances in which the interpreter overtly takes on his/her own persona in what is ostensibly a two-sided exchange between two other people. (Does this affect Deaf people's access to justice? Well, remember, it suits the court to believe that the interpreter is an input-output robot. And remember, the interpreter would not be there but for the Deaf person. So if the interpreter has a problem and becomes 'present', i.e. the robot fails, then in the court's eyes, the root of the problem is somehow connected to the Deaf person.)

Instances in which the interpreter becomes present may include the following (cf. Berk-Seligson 1990:55–96).

Direct address. Someone may address the interpreter directly—e.g., "Please ask him how many books he stole."

Anticipating interjection. The interpreter may interject to anticipate a misunderstanding—e.g. "I don't think I made the question clear"—or to block an irrelevant answer—e.g. "The defendant has responded, but he doesn't understand the question, so his answer doesn't make sense."

Clarification request. The interpreter may interject to clarify what someone is saying—e.g. "Could you be more specific about the weapon, because it is hard for me..." This may easily be seen as incompetence, an attempt to criticise the speaker's lack of clarity, or an unwarranted taking control of part of the exchange.

Explanation for approval. The interpreter may interject to explain his/her interpretation: in effect, a way of seeking approval or confirmation from the court that his/her behaviour is acceptable—e.g. "I asked him if he was in contact with his extended family, and I added 'aunts, uncles, grandparents, et cetera.'"

Signed aside. The interpreter may address 'side comments', in a language that the court as a whole cannot access, to the witness/defendant—e.g. when the witness interrupts a rambling section of explanation by the lawyer, signing 'not true, not true!', and the interpreter responds (in the midst of signing the lawyer's words) 'tell him, not me!'

Indicating direct address. The interpreter may draw attention to what is happening if the witness makes comments directly to the interpreter—e.g. by saying "He says he doesn't understand the question, and he asks me if I understand it."

Unless some strategy (e.g. switching to consecutive interpreting) is found to ensure otherwise, these points are significant because they mark clear instances where the proceedings are absolutely not parallel for both linguistic groups. The co-construction of the discourse is therefore altered: linguistically, something with considerable 'spin' is happening here.

In considering extreme examples of instances where the interpreter makes a self-generated contribution to the interaction, there emerges a sense of the interpreter as the very antithesis of robotic. It becomes apparent that the interpreter is pivotal to the interaction, and in a very real sense is in fact holding the entire conversation alone! After all, it is the interpreter's question that gets answered, and the interpreter's answer that prompts and conditions the next question. Everyone else is left to assume—and they do assume—that they are all engaged in a dialogue with each other, and that they both have access to the same dialogue. This may or may not be the case. In a setting such as a courtroom, where the whole event and its entire process consist of talking, the contribution the interpreter makes towards deciding the direction of the whole undertaking should not be underestimated. The implications of this deserve careful attention.[6]

Conclusions

The 1990s have seen something of a surge in attention to issues relating to language and the law. The first issue of a new journal, *Forensic Linguistics*, has appeared and commences with a valuable synthesis of some of the field's concerns (Levi 1994). A number of major collections have recently been made available (Levi & Graffam Walker 1990, Rieber and Stewart 1990, Gibbons 1994) which are likely to become primary resources. However, it has also been noted (e.g. by Tiersma 1993) that linguistic research on the law may remain underused by the legal profession because linguists are not always attuned to issues that other professionals find significant. Perhaps it is therefore worth attempting directly to highlight some of the practicable implications of the preceding discussion.

A number of pointers towards addressing some of the issues raised in this paper can briefly be set out here. These strategies will not be put into practice overnight: in fact—at least in respect of some of them— one would be wary if they were. The pressure to act now—to get more interpreters quickly, to make everyone aware of what it means to use an interpreter quickly—is so intense that the trade-off of speed against care favours short-cuts and feel-good solutions. This is a false economy: the fact that you can measure its effects in the short term does not mean that an answer is the best available. Instant remedies to profound problems may have propaganda value at best, whilst at worst papering over architecturally fundamental cracks. This point has been unequivocally made by Laster (1990:30):

"One political danger of quick-fix solutions is that they create the illusion that a problem has been 'fixed'. Yet, in practice they allow government to abdicate responsibility for often more important reforms. Interpreting may be necessary for the community to see that justice is done but the presence of an interpreter will not guarantee that justice is in fact achieved. To ignore this does serious injustice to interpreters and non-English speakers."

The plain truth is that we do not yet know how best to face all of the challenges outlined above. We may have to accept that some of the issues pose insoluble problems. In discussion of bilingual spoken language courtrooms, Morris (1989a:31) argues:

> "The basic dilemma of court interpretation results from the double need for on the one hand dynamism in interaction, and on the other the utmost accuracy in rendering material."

This seems to present as much, if not even more, of a dilemma in the situations dealt with in the present volume. It may simply be necessary to stop trying to navigate around the cartography of the bilingual, bimodal courtroom as if one could use the same old map: perhaps this is a fundamentally different landscape. It would seem that essential features of any programme of improvements to the status quo in this field should include the following elements.

Awareness

It does seem vital from the foregoing that participants in bilingual, bimodal courtroom interaction should be made aware of the possible outcomes of the linguistic situation that brings the interpreter into the picture. Amongst many possible elements, this should include anticipation, in instructions to participants, of any unavoidable properties of the interpreter's input which might unduly influence decisions: Kathy Laster cites a number of studies arguing that the court system as a whole needs much greater awareness of the linguistic problems inherent in the process of interpretation (Laster 1990:19). It should also include attempts to ensure that discipline (in the sense of Morris 1989a:33) is maintained over turntaking and delivery. Thirdly, it is crucial that allowances are made for the additional preparation required by all parties if the interpreting is to be maximally effective.[7] Overall, justice will only be served by a wider understanding that this is a hugely complex set of issues.

> "Legal training needs to be expanded beyond simply 'recipe-like' formulae on 'how to work with an interpreter' to incorporate a self-conscious awareness in lawyers of their objectives in questioning

witnesses and the impact which an interpreter might have on their approach." (Laster 1990:29)

Provision, recording and monitoring

In a number of countries, calls for legislation regarding statutory provision of interpreting services where necessary have now been heeded. Of course, in the absence of official recognition of national signed languages as equivalent in all relevant respects to spoken languages, it may be a moot point as to whether such legislation can be made to apply in the case of Deaf people. Together, these thus become primary goals for any attempt to address apparent shortcomings in the system of provision. Where these are in place, the secondary goal must be to press for certain guarantees of competence in the interpreting. Berk-Seligson reports (1990:216) that, with a failure rate of 96%, no test in the USA is as stringent as the federal certification exam for court interpreters: this is surely laudable. An appropriately comprehensive general education in interpreting may be a first stage: a demand for specialist situation-specific training should not be far behind. Attention ought also to be paid to working conditions for interpreters, covering such matters as the length of time for which one interpreter can reasonably be expected to work alone without mental fatigue detrimental to the functioning of the court.

Due process of law, in the event of an appeal concerning interpretation, cannot be guaranteed by an accurate record of court proceedings, but it is unquestionably impossible in its absence. Only if original testimony in both languages being used in the courtroom is recorded can material be compared, analysed and verified so as to ensure that honest and effective work has been done. As yet, however, not only is there no record whatsoever of any original signed material in the bimodal court in England, Wales and Northern Ireland, but the 1981 Contempt of Court Act actively disbars video-recording equipment from the courtroom. In the current climate of fair concern over standards as sign language interpreting emerges as a profession, this is a dangerous state of affairs that serves nobody well.

Recording of proceedings is imperative in order to substantiate any subsequent claims or appeals: as Berk-Seligson notes (1990:217), the provision of checks of this order can be seen as one test of the seriousness of the commitment the system is prepared to make to due process for the non-English speaking. At the actual time of trial, too, the introduction of basic checks and balances would contribute greatly to the cause of justice. No interpreter should be expected to work in a court of law in which he or she alone is able to gauge the accuracy and efficacy of his or her contributions. However competent that interpreter may be, he or she is also human and may make errors. Monitoring is a vital safeguard and must be carried out by trained persons able to recognise the difference between a finely judged question of interpretation and one of genuine and potentially significant mismatch between an original and an interpreter's rendition.

Training

As Morris (1989b:10) makes most explicit;

> "legislation dealing with the provision of interpretation does not necessarily of itself guarantee the high-quality interpretation which is a sine qua non for the exercising of the rights thus recognized".

High-level education and training of bimodal interpreters is a relatively recent phenomenon.[8] From the foregoing discussion, it can be seen that the ability to attend to detail and know how to respond appropriately in the complex legal milieu cannot become firmly rooted overnight. To function with anything like truly adequate competence, interpreters must be expected to have the greatest possible general command of the two languages involved, and to know the cultural ground in which they are embedded inside out, as well as possessing knowledge of the stylistic and content norms of the courtroom. Understanding of the operational patterns of the court's business must also be developed so that the interpreter is comfortably familiar with the events unfolding around him or her. Such understanding must be genuinely profound; as Laster (1990:29) puts it,

> "Interpreters need to be made aware of the complexities of the legal

system itself, not just the procedures and practices which they are likely to encounter."

In addition, whilst interpreting roles are clearly undergoing reassessment in this field, interpreters should be trained in such a way that they know as well as can be what is required of them, how they should aim to conduct themselves, and the limits of the flexibility and responsiveness to circumstances available to them.

Research

Finally, in the context of a field acknowledged to be so well-endowed with unknowns, primary research of all kinds must continue to be a priority. Approximately 35 years of sign linguistic research have produced a number of major analyses yielding a great deal of significant information concerning the elements and structures of signed languages. Nevertheless, the gaps in understanding and codification continue to be wide and much rests on scholars' collective ability to generate accounts of grammar, lexis and patterns of usage which can form the basis for other types of progress.

Research into interpreting as a process and a practice is also vital in order to expand understanding of both internal (cognitive) and external (interactional) strategies which can produce optimal performance of interpreting duties in the intense, multi-layered environment of the courtroom. Controlled experimental research, ethnographic work and action research can all be seen to have considerable contributions to make to the evolution of ever richer and more detailed descriptive and explanatory accounts. These should in turn provide suitable material for application to address the issues identified above.

Acknowledgments

This paper owes much to contributions from Susan Berk-Seligson, Mary Brennan, David Brien, Richard Brown, Ester Chu, Diana Eades, Kyra Pollitt, Maureen Reed, Cynthia Roy, Douglas Silas, and Cecilia Wadensjö, as well as all of the contributors to the volume in which it was originally published and individual interpreters interviewed in the course of research. Nobody but the author bears any responsibility for the finished product. The project acknowledges the support of the Leverhulme Trust, ASLI, SASLI, CACDP, BDA and RAD and the generous co-operation of Glasgow and West of Scotland Society for the Deaf, Strathclyde Regional Council and St. Vincent's Society for the Deaf in Glasgow.

Notes

1. This paper was first presented to the American Association for Applied Linguistics in 1994 and benefited enormously from discussion with members of the audience on that occasion.
2. Under the direction of Dr. Mary Brennan and Professor Richard Brown, the author was, at the time of writing, engaged in such a programme of research. Entitled Access to Justice for Deaf People in the Bilingual, Bimodal Courtroom, the programme was supported by the Leverhulme Trust.
3. It must be clearly stated that this study could not have come together without the co-operation of organisations in the field, including the Association of Sign Language Interpreters (ASLI), the Scottish Association of Sign Language Interpreters (SASLI), the Council for the Advancement of Communication with Deaf People (CACDP), the British Deaf Association (BDA) and the Royal Association in aid of Deaf People (RAD). Individual correspondents, and persons named in examples of court interaction, are not identified for reasons of confidentially.
4. The capital 'D' here is adopted-following a convention proposed by James Woodward (1972) and developed by Carol Padden (1980)-to refer to members of the sign language using cultural minority group.
5. See Brennan et al (1984) and Brien (1992) for an explanation of the researcher's notation system which is used as a tool of linguistic analysis; and Thoutenhoofd (1990, 1992) for a comparison of writing systems and notation systems.
6. Some initial attempts to draw out these implications can be found in Turner and Brown (this volume).
7. A key example of this requirement being taken seriously would be the European Court of Justice where (Heidelberger 1994:3-4) interpreters are allowed "ample study time to ensure that [they] are well

prepared and familiar with the facts of the individual case, the legal issues involved and the working of the court in general."

8 In the UK, the first postgraduate British Sign Language/English Interpreting course was established at the University of Durham in 1988.

References

Anthony, D. (1971). *Seeing Essential English*, 1 and 2. Educational Services Division: Anaheim CA.

Bergman, B. (1979). *Signed Swedish*. National Swedish Board of Education: Stockholm.

Berk-Seligson, S. (1990). *The Bilingual Courtroom: Court Interpreters in the Judicial Process*. Chicago University Press: Chicago IL and London.

Bornstein, H. et al. (1975). *The Signed English Dictionary for preschool and elementary levels*. Gallaudet College Press: Washington DC.

Brennan, M., Colville, M., Lawson, L. K. and Hughes, G. S. M. (1984). *Words in Hand: A Structural Analysis of the Signs of British Sign Language* (second edition). Moray House College of Education: Edinburgh.

Brennan, M. (1986). Linguistic Perspectives. In B. T. Tervoort (ed.), *Signs of Life: Proceedings of the Second European Congress on Sign Language Research*. NSDSK/Institute of General Linguistics, University of Amsterdam/Dutch Council of the Deaf: Amsterdam. 1–16.

—— (1992). The Visual World of BSL: An Introduction. In Brien, D. (ed) *Dictionary of British Sign Language/English*. Faber and Faber: London and Boston MA. 1–133.

Brien, D. (ed.) (1992). *Dictionary of British Sign Language/English*. Faber and Faber: London and Boston MA.

Butler, I. and Noaks, L. (1992). Silence in Court? A Study of Interpreting in the Courts of England and Wales. School of Social and Administrative Studies, University of Wales College of Cardiff/London: Nuffield Interpreter Project.

Caccamise, F., Oglia, D., Mitchell, M., DeGroote, W. and Siple, L. (1991). *Technical Signs Manual Eleven: Legal*. RIT/NTID: New York NY.

Cameron, D. (1994). Putting our Practice into Theory. In D. Graddol and J. Swann (eds.), *Evaluating Language*. Clevedon, British Association for Applied Linguistics in association with Multilingual Matters: Avon and Bristol PA. 15–23.

Cameron, D., Frazer, E., Harvey, P., Rampton, M. B. H. and Richardson, K. (1992). *Researching Language: Issues of Power and Method*. Routledge: London and New York NY.

CACDP (no date). *Curriculum and Assessment Procedures-Stage 1*. CACDP: Durham.

Crystal, D. and Davy, D. (1969). *Investigating English Style*. Longman: London.

Danet, B. (1980). Language in the legal process. *Law and Society Review*, 14:445–564.

Eades, D. (1988). Sociolinguistic evidence in court. *Australian Journal of Communication*, 14: 22–31.

—— (1992). Australian Aborigines and the Legal System: A Sociolinguistic Perspective. Paper presented at Sociolinguistics Symposium 9. University of Reading, England.

Gibbons, J. (ed.) (1994). *Language and the law*. Longman: London and New York NY.

Giles, H. (1970). Evaluative reactions to accents. *Educational Review*, 22:211–227.

—— (1971). Ethnocentrism and the evaluation of accented speech. *British Journal of Social and Clinical Psychology*, 10:187–188.

Goodwin, C. (1994) Narrative co-construction in the family of an aphasic. Paper presented to the American Association for Applied Linguistics 'Co-Construction' Colloquium. Baltimore MD.

Gustason, G., Pfetzing, D. and Zawolkow, E. (1975). *Signing Exact English*. Modern Signs Press: Los Alamitos CA.

Harness Goodwin, M. (1994). Co-constructed participation frameworks in a multi-ethnic classroom. Paper presented to the American Association for Applied Linguistics 'Co-Construction' Colloquium. Baltimore MD.

Heidelberger, B. (1994). Legal Interpreting: The Example of the Court of Justice of the European Communities. *The Jerome Quarterly*, 9/3:3–15.

HMSO (1993). *Report of the Royal Commission on Criminal Justice*. HMSO: London.

Islam, M. (1993). Read, Hear, See... "See Hear!" Read...! *NEWSLI*, 14:30–31.

Jaworski, A. (1993). *Power of Silence: Social and Pragmatic Perspectives*. Sage: London.

Lane, H. (1992). *The Mask of Benevolence: Disabling the Deaf Community.* Alfred A. Knopf: New York NY.

Laster, K. (1990). Legal interpreters: conduits to social justice? *Journal of Intercultural Studies,* 11/2:15–32.

Levi, J. (1994). Language as evidence: the linguist as expert witness in North American courts. *Forensic Linguistics,* 1/1:1–26.

Levi, J. and Graffam Walker, A. (eds.) (1990). *Language in the judicial process.* Plenum: New York NY.

Lightbown, P. (1994) Teachers and Researchers: Both Oars in the Water. Plenary Paper to the American Association for Applied Linguistics. Baltimore MD.

Lochrie, Rev J. S. (no date). *Notes for Interpreters for the Deaf in Courts of Law in Scotland.* Moray House College of Education: Edinburgh.

Loftus, E. and Palmer, J. (1974). Reconstruction of automobile destruction: An example of the interaction between language and memory. *Journal of Verbal Learning and Verbal Behaviour,* 13:585–589.

Loftus, E. and Zanni, G. (1975). Eyewitness testimony: Influence of the wording of a question. *Bulletin of the Psychonomic Society,* 5:86–88.

McIntire, M. and Sanderson, G. (in press). Bye-bye, bi-bi: Questions of empowerment and role. In *Proceedings,* 1993 RID Convention.

Morris, R. (1989a). Court Interpretation: The Trial of Ivan Demjanjuk: A Case Study. *The Interpreters' Newsletter,* 2:27–37.

—— (1989b). Eichmann v. Demjanjuk: A Study of Interpreted Proceedings. *Parallèles: Cahiers de L'Ecole de Traduction et d'Interpretation,* Université de Genève. 9–28.

Nuffield Interpreter Project (1993). *Access to Justice: Non-English Speakers in the Legal System.* The Nuffield Foundation: London.

Nusser, P. (1993). Acting upon your beliefs. *TBC News,* 63:4.

O'Barr, W. (1982). *Linguistic Evidence: Language, Power, and Strategy in the Courtroom.* Academic Press: New York NY.

Padden, C. (1980) The Deaf Community and the Culture of Deaf People. In C. Baker and R. Battison (eds.), *Sign Language and the Deaf Community: Essays in Honour of William C. Stokoe.* National Association of the Deaf: Silver Spring MD. 89–104.

Padden, C. and Humphries, T. (1988). *Deaf in America: Voices from a Culture.* Harvard University Press: Cambridge MA.

Parker, D. (1993). Mixed-up sentences. *The Guardian*. London. February 2nd.

Polack, K. and Corsellis, A. (1990). Non-English speakers and the criminal justice system. *New Law Journal*, November 23rd:1634–1677.

Rieber, R. and Stewart, W. (eds.) (1990). *The language scientist as expert in the legal setting: Issues in forensic linguistics*. New York Academy of Sciences: New York NY.

Roy, C. (1989). A Sociolinguistic Analysis of the Interpreter's Role in the Turn Exchanges of an Interpreted Event. Unpublished dissertation. Washington DC: Georgetown University, University Microfilms DAO64793.

—— (1993a). The Problem with Definitions, Descriptions, and the Role Metaphors of Interpreters. *Journal of Interpretation*, 6/1:127–153.

—— (1993b). A sociolinguistic analysis of the interpreter's role in simultaneous talk in interpreted interaction. *Multilingua*, 12/4:341–363.

Schegloff, E. (1994). On the co-construction of discourse: The omnirelevance of action. Paper presented to the American Association for Applied Linguistics 'Co-Construction' Colloquium. Baltimore MD.

Scott Gibson, L. (1990). Sign Language Interpreting: An Emerging Profession. In S. Gregory and G. M. Hartley (eds.), (1991). *Constructing Deafness*. Pinter Publishers in association with the Open University: London/Milton Keynes: 253–258.

—— (1994). Open to Interpretation: The Cult of Professionalism. Keynote paper presented at the 'Issues in Interpreting' Conference. University of Durham, England.

Sutton-Spence, R. and Woll, B. (1990). Variation and recent change in British Sign Language. *Language Variation and Change*, 2.:313–330.

—— (1993). The Status and Functional Role of Fingerspelling in BSL. IM. Marschark and M. D. Clark (eds.), *Psychological Perspectives on Deafness*. Lawrence Erlbaum Associates: Hillsdale NJ. 185–208.

Thoutenhoofd, E.D. (1990). The link between calligraphy and notation, or: why type-designing is a job for type-designers. *Signpost*, 3/1:12–13.

—— (1992). Trans-scribing and writing: What constitutes a writing system? *Signpost*, 5/2:39–51.

Tiersma, P. (1993). Review article: Linguistic issues in the law. *Language*, 69/1:113–137.

Turner, G. H. and Brown, R. K. (this volume).

Wadensjö, C. (1992). *Interpreting as Interaction*. Linköping University: Linköping.

Witter-Merithew, A. (1986). Claiming our destiny. (In two parts). *RID Views*. October:12 and November:3–4.

Woodward, J. (1972) Implications for sociolinguistic research among the deaf. *Sign Language Studies*, 1:1–7.

# Interaction and the role of the interpreter in court
Graham H. Turner and Richard K. Brown

Introduction

In this paper, we consider the interactional role of the British Sign Language/English interpreter in mediating the proceedings of the bilingual, bimodal courtroom. Noting the social and linguistic complexity of such events, we look at the role currently expected for interpreters working between signed and spoken languages. Taking the point of view that the interpreter's performance will be pivotal to the success and efficiency of communication, and thus to the quality of the judicial process carried out, we make a case for a re-appraisal of the role specified for the interpreter in courtroom interaction. This is an exploratory paper, both because sign linguistics is still a relatively young discipline and because our project (entitled *Access to Justice for Deaf People in the Bilingual, Bimodal Courtroom*) is still at a very early stage.

The project

The services of a BSL/English interpreter are essential if Deaf people are to have fair and proper treatment when they appear in court as defendants or witnesses. But court interpreting is an inherently complex process and some fine interpreters refuse to touch it because it makes such special demands. The objectives of the project are to explore the access of Deaf people to justice within the courts, the role of BSL/English interpreters in mediating such access, the problems inherent in the process of interpreting courtroom discourse, and the socio-cultural influences on the nature of courtroom interactions. The outcomes from this study will feed into both interpreter training and, ultimately, it is hoped, into policy-making with respect to justice and the Deaf community.

We are concerned with the experience of Deaf people within the criminal justice process in general, and with the interactions which take place within the courtroom in particular. Thus, the project has three

Paper given at INI2, the second *Issues in Interpreting* conference. Durham University, 19 September 1995.

main parts: firstly, to gather and collate evidence from records and interviews with Deaf people, interpreters and others about experiences in the criminal justice process, and the roles which interpreters play; secondly, to record and analyse courtroom interaction in cases where a BSL/English interpreter is working; and thirdly, to work towards developing training materials and programmes, guidelines about good practice and academic reports of the research findings.

Background

Let us now attempt to put the question of court interpreting into some kind of context. Why is this an important area to study? We live in an age when the public conscience seems regularly to be faced with examples of the failure of our legal system to be effective and accountable, resulting in a spate of widely reported miscarriages of justice (Mansfield 1993). The European Convention on Human Rights includes the provision—and similar principles are embedded in legislation in this country—that anyone charged with a criminal offence has the right to be informed in detail, and in a language which he or she understands, about the accusation made against him or her. It is accepted that this needs to happen in a language which he or she understands and that the free assistance of interpreter may be needed in order to achieve this aim.

In 1993, a judgement in the European Court of Human Rights suggested that the individual right to interpreting extends beyond the face-to-face interaction to include translations of written documents and makes those providing an interpreter responsible for the standard and competence of the service provided (Nuffield Interpreter Project 1993:5). Cases suggesting that these provisions are not always met within the UK have recently been highlighted (ibid). In fact, one survey found that there was no universally accepted formal process for checking any aspect of an interpreter's competence; and that only a half or fewer of the courts using interpreters took steps to ensure such competence (Butler and Noaks 1992).

In many respects, the situation with respect to BSL/English interpreting is probably markedly better than for most linguistic minorities in the UK. There are national registers of interpreters and police forces keep their own lists for police interviews. On the Metropolitan Police list, for example, interpreters' level of qualification—from fully qualified interpreter to sign language beginner—is recorded alongside contact details. However, those responsible will sometimes simply continue down the list until they find someone who is free, without further consideration of the consequences of employing an unqualified interpreter. Thus it is possible that someone with a Stage 1 certificate in BSL—a language skills certificate, not an interpreting award—based on 60 hours of teaching and an examination of about 15 minutes, might be called upon to interpret within the criminal justice process. Even fully qualified interpreters are by no means necessarily highly-trained legal specialists. At the time of writing, the only established training course in legal interpreting for BSL/English interpreters lasts five days, and its specifically linguistic content consists of 'vocabulary development sessions'.

Elsewhere in this volume (*The Bilingual, Bimodal Courtroom: A First Glance*), language issues arising when Deaf people encounter the legal system are outlined for exploration against a back-drop of the wider analysis of bilingual courtrooms. In the remainder of this paper, the focus is firmly upon the interactional role of the interpreter and how it shapes the communicative process.

The interpreter's role

If a rolling programme of re-evaluation of the interpreting role had been designed as the profession began to emerge, it could scarcely have been more animated than the informal process which has developed within the field. In recent years, one can see policy-makers and theorists in the sign language field attempting to tackle the feeling that the models enshrined in Codes of Practice and Codes of Ethics are fundamentally flawed (Witter-Merithew 1986, Roy 1989a, 1993a, 1993b, Frishberg 1990, Baker-Shenk 1991, Scott Gibson 1991).

Essentially, there seems to be a growing consensus that trainers' and practitioners' interpretations of the role as prescribed have been subject to certain weaknesses. For most of the first two-thirds of this century, interpreting with Deaf people was unregulated, uncontrolled and unrecognised as a professional occupation. The result too often was a well-meaning but ultimately disempowering tendency for the 'interpreter' to act on behalf of the Deaf person rather than facilitating that person's own actions (this stance is sometimes referred to as the *helper* model). When the profession began to emerge, the regulations laid down were seen to impose a highly mechanistic approach (or *conduit* model) in order to disengage as far as possible from the history of 'interpreters' over-stepping the boundaries of personal involvement in Deaf people's lives.

The result is an image of the interpreter as a wholly *passive* channel through which the messages of primary participants pass. The current *Code of Practice* in force in England, Wales and Northern Ireland (CACDP, 1993:2–5) contains only one direct instruction concerning such issues. It is unequivocal:

1. Interpreters shall interpret truly and faithfully to the best of their ability between the parties *without anything being added or omitted* (our italics).

The Council for the Advancement of Communication with Deaf People includes in its Directory the following information (CACDP, 1993:2–2) on using interpreters:

Role of the interpreter
The interpreter's job is to pass messages from people using British Sign Language to English and vice versa. Interpreters will use their skill and knowledge of the two different languages and cultures to pass on the same message but using a different language.
Interpreters may sometimes stop to ask the speaker (*sic*) for the message to be repeated if it is unclear to them or if they have missed something. Otherwise the interpreter should not interrupt or get involved in the conversation.
Interpreters must follow the CACDP *Code of Practice* and are expected to be impartial, unobtrusive and to keep confidential everything they interpret.

Thus both the Code of Practice and the guidelines are heavily influenced by conduit model notions. The important points in the present context are the apparently strict stipulations about when the interpreter is at liberty to contribute something not generated by one of the principal participants.

Many interpreters knowingly but guiltily break the rules—because their hearts tell them that their interpretations are the better for it—and then wonder whether they have done the right thing. Cynthia Roy indicates that conflicting interpretations of the conduit-style guidelines have persisted since at least the early 1970s (1989:92–94), with the result that interpreters working with Deaf people have suffered a profound unease about the limits of their professional practice for some twenty years.

> While these metaphors clearly are responding to a need, they also carry double messages. On the one hand, these descriptions attempt to convey the difficulty of simultaneous tasks in interpreting while reminding everyone that the interpreter is uninvolved on any other level; at the same time, the same descriptions encourage interpreters to be flexible, which usually means to be involved. While descriptions and standards of ethical practice extensively, sometimes exhaustively, list what interpreters should not do, they seldom, if ever, explain what interpreters can do, that is, explain what "flexible" means. Consequently, no one really knows where to draw the line on the involvement of the interpreter. (Roy 1993a:134, cf. Wadensjö 1992:33)

The confusion is both reported by practitioners (McIntire and Sanderson 1994) and evident in the literature. Nancy Frishberg (1990) begins to address the sense of inadequacy of the mechanistic approach, arguing that the conduit model denies the human qualities of the interpreter.[1] Yet Frishberg still advances some apparently incompatible views. Having clearly acknowledged the value of the interpreter taking a role as a participant in interaction (1990:27-28), Frishberg nevertheless goes on to cite with approval work which emphasises that the interpreter "will work best when least noticed by the participants" (1990:61).

In the light of recent linguistic research into the interactional matter of interpreted events, however, it seems that there are good grounds for a significant shift in approach. Wherever Codes of Practice or Ethics stipulate that the interpreter must play no part in the exchange save to relay messages from one party to the other and back, an element of unrealistic idealism has crept into the role norms. For an interpreter-mediated exchange is *inescapably* multi-party in nature. Current models of 'the best of all interpreted worlds' tend to direct readers to expect the interpreter to be utterly unobtrusive and the event to continue as if it were monolingual. This is not, and cannot actually be, the case.

The contribution of interactional sociolinguistics

The concept of *co-construction*, or 'discourse as an interactional achievement', is currently enjoying attention from scholars such as Charles Goodwin (1994), Marjorie Harness Goodwin (1994) and Emmanuel Schegloff (1994) as a central process in social life. Co-construction is conceived as a joining together of participants in the joint production and interpretation of utterances, ideas, and so on. One of the central implications of the idea is that *meaning* in talk cannot be something that one person does by themself: meaning is *created between* producers and perceivers, speakers and hearers. In the interpreted situation, therefore, three parties' efforts are engaged as meanings are developed and distributed between producer, intermediary and perceiver.

This general principle has been recognised by a number of interpreting theorists to have a potentially major contribution to make to our understanding of interpreting principles and practice. Cynthia Roy completed a study in 1989 (describing the self-generated contributions to interaction made by a conscientious ASL-English interpreter in order to enable communication to be effective between the principal participants) which, she concludes;

> shows that an interpreted event is an exchange of talk between three people, all of whom are actively contributing to the direction and outcome of the event. (Roy 1989:259)

Roy's analysis shows that interpreters participate in a series of functional ways if they are truly going to bridge the communication gap; once they do so, they become "members of interpreted conversations" (1993b:360) in their own right. How does this manifest itself in the courtroom? A question is posed by the prosecution to a witness: but the question to which the witness actually responds is the one posed by the interpreter. The answer comes back from the witness: but the answer that the court will use in reaching judgement and in the light of which the prosecuting counsel frames the next question is the one given by the interpreter. Far from being a mere conduit, the interpreter is the person who participates directly in every interactional turn.

Support for this view is beginning to appear in the wider field. Roy's descriptions are based on research involving interpreter-mediated conversation between an ASL-user and an English-speaker. From her study of Swedish-Russian spoken language interpreting, Cecilia Wadensjö develops a number of complementary conclusions. In particular, Wadensjö (1992:102–113) gives a detailed account of the "explicit co-ordinating moves", i.e. self-generated turns designed to permit the efficient management of dialogue, that make the interpreter 'visible' and very much present as an interactant. In this way, adopting the perspective of the interactional sociolinguist, Wadensjö is able to work with great rigour beyond the conduit approach (whereby the interpreter merely relays others' contributions back and forth) towards a potential new metaphor for the interpreter's role:

> When the interpreter's role performance is investigated as interaction [...] it becomes self-evident that the dialogue interpreter must be conceived of as both relayer and co-ordinator. Consequently, an adequate description of difficulties and possibilities in being a dialogue interpreter demands an account not only of the translating (relaying) aspect but also of the co-ordinating aspect of her task. (Wadensjö, 1992:266)

A role in interaction?

Looking back at Nancy Frishberg's discussion of the limits of the interpreter's role now becomes an extremely revealing exercise. Here's what Frishberg—and with her a whole generation of interpreter trainers for whom her introductory volume was the primary resource—said (1990:67) about the interpreter as participant:[2]

> At least three undesired outcomes are more likely when the interpreter participates [...]
> First, the interpreter becomes responsible for the outcome of the interaction [...].
> Secondly [...] he or she encourages the deaf and hearing people to

become dependent on the interpreter [...]
Thirdly [...] the next interpreter may not be so [...] desirous of involvement. The clients will have an altogether inconsistent or incorrect notion of what an interpreter's role and function are if the professionals do not hold to a firm policy of non-involvement.

Let us take these in reverse order. The third 'undesired outcome' occurs as a direct consequence of the regulations in force and the way in which trainees are enculturated into adopting them. It is, in this sense, a technicality that can legitimately be defined away if the role and the rules governing it were to be amended. If the co-ordinator role were to be inscribed into the Codes of Practice and Ethics, professionals would be required to have a firm policy of involvement in order to fulfil their function consistently and correctly. This outcome is therefore readily open to adjustment since it is a matter of procedure or structure rather than of principle.

The second 'undesired outcome' is more fundamental. Yet there is evidence of a swing away from the dyed-in-the-wool view that dependency of any kind is necessarily a bad thing in this context. McIntire and Sanderson (personal communication), for instance, advocate a stance according to which:

> the interpreter does not view the [...] consumer as incompetent, but rather *temporarily* unable to do for him- or herself. For us, this makes all the difference.

This point of view has evolved as part of a reappraisal of the notion of power in relation to the interpreter. In the context of the prevalence of the helper model of interpreting, it was important to reflect in Codes of Practice and Ethics Deaf people's right to lead their own lives without interference. This grew to be seen as a declaration that interpreters must not have *power* over consumers, so that consumers could be permitted to maintain their independence. Hindsight suggests that a significant confusion between power and *control* knocked this construction awry (McIntire and Sanderson 1994). In practice—and as a matter of principle—interpreters are, by the very nature of the occupation, powerful in just the same way that a doctor is powerful: they're powerful because consumers need them to be so in order that they can work effectively in the consumers' interests (Baker-Shenk 1991; Turner, 1991). The suggestion that the interpreter be guided by revised guidelines to take an active role as a co-ordinator of interaction does nothing to undermine the independence of consumers: rather, it augments their capacity to engage in maximally effective and productive dialogue across language boundaries. Participation in this sense, then, should in no way be seen as undesirable.

Finally, what of the argument that the interpreter is afforded too much responsibility for the outcome of mediated exchanges unless the role is kept strictly in the conduit mould? The Code of Ethics developed by the Registry of Interpreters for the Deaf, Inc. in the USA explicitly states in its guidelines that responsibility for the outcome of communication "does not rightly belong" to the interpreter (Frishberg, 1990:197). Again, a real shift can be observed in the positions taken on this issue. Anna Witter-Merithew (1986:12) stands out as an early progressive thinker:

> [T]he one thing we have historically claimed the least responsibility [for]—the interpreted message—is the very thing over which we have most control.

This radical claim can be seen to have been refined with the benefit of both detailed analyses of what actually functions as good practice in the interpreter-mediated context, and the emerging concept of the interpreter as co-ordinator (Wadensjö 1992). Interpreters do not altogether bear responsibility for consumers getting just what they want as a result of dialogue: no-one is advocating a return to the 'let me do it for you' approach of the helper model. But interpreters do, it is argued, bear the responsibility for successfully *managing* and *negotiating* (i.e. co-ordinating) the communication event.

Returning to the concept of co-construction, the active engagement of the interpreter in achieving a satisfactory product from talk (i.e. jointly constructing a conversation in which the participants manage to understand each other) can now be seen in a different light. Moving away from the normative position taken by Nancy Frishberg, what emerges here is the suggestion that interpretation can be most effective when the interpreter is seen as a participant with a special co-ordinating function. From such a perspective, where the interpreter is licensed to make a particular contribution to the interaction, we get a sense of the interpreter as the very antithesis of mechanical. Rather, it becomes apparent that the interpreter is *pivotal* to the interaction.

The co-ordinator in the courtroom

And so we return to the courtroom. On the basis of the discussion so far, we are drawn to the view that a convergence of factors—the interactional complexity of the bilingual, bimodal courtroom and the apparently impending shift to a new model of the interpreting role in general—amount to an indication that the manner of participation of the BSL/English interpreter in court might constructively be reviewed.

Neither Susan Berk-Seligson nor Ruth Morris, who have provided the most thorough analyses of bilingual court interaction, are in any doubt about the participation status of the interpreter. Berk-Seligson categorically states (1990:96) that:

> [T]he court interpreter is a new variable in the ecology of the [...] courtroom. She is an intrusive element far from being the unobtrusive figure whom judges and attorneys would like her to be. Her intrusiveness is manifested in multiple ways [...] Together, these intrusions make for judicial proceedings of a different nature.

Berk-Seligson goes on to show, in immense detail (1990:146-197), that what the interpreter does, the way he or she does it and the choices he or she is obliged to make have a measurable effect on viewers and listeners. Morris (1989a:31–2) reaches a related conclusion, saying that interpreters in practice undertake:

> a role which is not limited exclusively to reproducing participants' utterances, and which may involve their exerting some degree of influence over the proceedings proper, including exercising control over speakers.

And yet the role norms attempt to disregard all of this as an irrelevance and pretend that the legal proceedings have not changed. The courtroom is attended by a range of people, each of whom have a part to play in the unfolding talk-event. To this extent alone, the interpreter's need to manage the exchange is probably greater here than in any other setting: this stressful aspect is compounded by an inescapable awareness of the gravity of the court's business and the consequent necessity for precision. The result is what Morris (1989a:31 and 1989b:10) calls the "basic dilemma" of court interpretation: both dynamism in interaction and the utmost accuracy in rendering material are utterly vital to the successful conclusion of the proceedings.

Marina McIntire and Gary Sanderson (1994) have pointed out two potentially damaging consequences to the interests of justice if bimodal interpreters are procedurally disabled from working effectively. On the one hand, they suggest that the interpreter who is uncomfortable and lacking in self-confidence[3] in court may well opt to fall back into the stance of the conduit in a bid to evade responsibility for his or her own performance. On the other hand, these authors report knowledge of interpreters—upon observing the damaging attitude the court adopts towards the Deaf person—resolving to conduct themselves as helpers of the Deaf person, even to the extent of lying, changing testimony and asking leading questions.

In attempting to address this situation, then, we would raise the suggestion that a change of emphasis in interpreting Codes of Practice and Ethics would be of particular benefit to the interests of justice as pursued in court interaction. The shift proposed would aim to enable interpreters to accept responsibility for managing and thus literally facilitating communication. Crucially, it would aim not to define away but to control the interpreter's input to the interaction. It would seek neither to give the interpreter free rein to interfere in the principal participants' affairs, nor to prevent the interpreter being effective by imposing a blanket ban on self-generated contributions, but to limit those contributions to matters of interactional co-ordination and management. As Cynthia Roy says (1993a:139), the division between the helper and conduit metaphors hinges on the distinction between "extreme personal involvement and extreme to not-so-extreme non-involvement of the interpreter." Somewhere between these two extremes, there is a position that should actively enhance effective communication between primary interactants whilst acknowledging some of the vital human qualities of the person in the middle. It is imperative that we recognise and do not lose sight of the fact that the interpreter must play an active role in achieving communication. Once this is acknowledged, we can begin to make it a source of strength and confidence rather than weakness and guilt:

> All communication is an interactive exchange, and when interpreters are used, they are a part of the interaction naturally. The point is not their neutrality but rather what is or can be their participation in the event. (Roy 1989:265)

Conclusions

Whether or not the ideas put forward in this paper are well received, it is vital to note that the conduit model of legal interpreting is plainly a fiction, convenient for the system, but replete with unwelcome consequences for the legal profession, the human rights of Deaf people and the proper administration of justice.[4] Nevertheless, it may be that in the longer term, solutions more radical than adjusting Codes of Practice and Ethics will be seen as the most effective way forward.

One such approach is advocated by Kathy Laster (1990:17). In the absence of a realistic understanding of what an interpreter must and can do within the limits of his or her role, she argues, the law makes ambiguous and contradictory demands of interpreters. Consequently, non-English speakers are not always better off when an interpreter is used.

> The issue whether to use an interpreter in individual cases therefore is better conceived of as a tactical one rather than as an abstract question of 'rights'. The advantage of this approach is that it focuses attention on the aspects of the legal system itself which militate against social justice for non-English speakers rather than allowing interpreters to be regarded as 'the problem' requiring 'reform'.

Even more daring, or perhaps desperate, is the stand taken by the Freedom of Choice movement in Canada which, according to Berk-Seligson (1990:215), has concluded that it is prejudicial to the defendant's interests to have the trial interpreted for him or her, since accuracy cannot be guaranteed. The group therefore claims the right to a trial conducted in a language that the defendant understands. In an appeal in February 1988, the Canadian Supreme Court's response was that the defendant had no such right. Which, if any, of these lines of action will prove beneficial to interpreters, Deaf people and the legal systems of the UK? The case, as they say, continues.

Epilogue

Early in April 1995, subsequent to first presentation of this paper, the Council for the Advancement of Communication with Deaf People in the UK launched a new 'Code of Ethics for Sign Language Interpreters' in England, Wales and Northern ireland. Taking on board concerns expressed to the Working Party responsible for the new Code—a working party that invited comment and constructive criticism of the existing Code throughout an extensive consultation exercise—this document does in fact indicate a wish to specifiy a more interactively engaged role for the BSL/English interpreter.

In particular, item two of the new Code reads (note the extra three words at the end here):

2   Interpreters shall interpret truly and faithfully and to the best of their ability between the parties without anything being added or omitted from the meaning.

Although there almost inevitably remain ambiguities and issues open to interpretation in this revised clause, it is nevertheless clear that the Working Party has grappled with the problem identified in this paper. Further, item seven reads:

7   Interpreters shall not give advice or offer personal opinions in relation to topics discussed or people present in an interpreting assignment.
i   It is a legitimate part of the interpreter's role to take appropriate steps to ensure good communication is facilitated between people who have different linguistic and cultural backgrounds. Such steps should always be taken in as professional and unobtrusive a manner as possible.

The effects of this shift in alignment within the Code remain to be seen and ongoing refinements are likely. From the point of view taken in this paper, it would seem that positive steps have been taken to enhance the significant contribution an interpreter may make to effective communication.

Acknowledgments

This paper owes much to the generosity in discussing relevant issues of Susan Berk-Seligson, Mary Brennan, David Brien, Esther Chu, Diana Eades, Marina McIntire, Clive Palmer, Kyra Pollitt, Maureen Reed, Cynthia Roy, Gary Sanderson, Douglas Silas and Cecilia Wadensjö, as well as all of the interpreters interviewed in the course of research. Nobody but the authors bears any responsibility for the finished product.

Notes

1. These terms are familiar in the UK in the writing of Liz Scott Gibson (1991:256–7).
2. Frishberg was focussing here on the issue of impartiality. It is perhaps indicative of the uncertainties about what needed to be said that these comments actually give some of the clearest directions available about participation in general.
3. Interview reports in the course of our *Access to Justice* project clearly indicate that such self-confidence is frequently actively undermined by legal professionals, including judges themselves.
4. A number of suggestions towards more procedural initiatives which arose in the course of work on the Durham project and are designed to enhance the secure efficiency of the bilingual, bimodal courtroom are set out elsewhere in this volume.

References

Baker-Shenk, C. (1991). The interpreter: Machine, advocate, or ally? *Expanding Horizons: Proceedings of the 1991 RID Convention*. RID Publications: Silver Spring MD. 120–140.

Berk-Seligson, S. (1990). *The Bilingual Courtroom: Court Interpreters in the Judicial Process*. Chicago University Press: Chicago and London.

CACDP (1993). *Directory*. CACDP: Durham.

Frishberg, N. (1990). *Interpreting: An Introduction (Revised edition)*. RID Publications: Silver Spring MD.

Goodwin, C. (1994) Narrative co-construction in the family of an aphasic. Paper presented to the American Association for Applied Linguistics 'Co-Construction' Colloquium. Baltimore MD.

Harness Goodwin, M. (1994). Co-constructed participation frameworks in a multi-ethnic classroom. Paper presented to the American Association for Applied Linguistics 'Co-Construction' Colloquium. Baltimore MD.

Heidelberger, B. (1994). Legal Interpreting: The Example of the Court of Justice of the European Communities. *The Jerome Quarterly*, 9/3:3–15.

Laster, K. (1990). Legal interpreters: conduits to social justice? *Journal of Intercultural Studies*, 11/2:15–32.

McIntire, M. and Sanderson, G. (1994). Who's in charge here? Perceptions of empowerment and role in the interpreter setting. Paper presented to the American Association for Applied Linguistics 'The Bilingual, Bimodal Courtroom' Colloquium, Baltimore MD.

Morris, R. (1989a). Court Interpretation: The Trial of Ivan Demjanjuk: A Case Study. *The Interpreters' Newsletter*, 2:27–37.

——(1989b). Eichmann v. Demjanjuk: A Study of Interpreted Proceedings. *Parallèles: Cahiers de l'École de Traduction et d'Interpretation, Université de Genève*. 9–28.

Roy, C. (1989). A Sociolinguistic Analysis of the Interpreter's Role in the Turn Exchanges of an Interpreted Event. Unpublished dissertation. Washington DC: Georgetown University, University Microfilms DAO64793.

——(1993a). The Problem with Definitions, Descriptions, and the Role Metaphors of Interpreters. *Journal of Interpretation*, 6/1:127–153.

——(1993b). A sociolinguistic analysis of the interpreter's role in simultaneous talk in interpreted interaction. *Multilingua*, 12/4:341–363.

Scott Gibson, L. (1991). Sign Language Interpreting: An Emerging Profession. In S. Gregory and G. M. Hartley (eds.), *Constructing Deafness*. Pinter Publishers in association with the Open University: London/Milton Keynes. 253–258.

Turner, G. H. (1991). Random Rantings. *Signpost*, 4:19.

Wadensjö, C. (1992). *Interpreting as Interaction*. Linsköping University: Linsköping.

Ward, C. (1994). Fringe Bene.ts. *New Statesman and Society*, 7/309:28.

Witter-Merithew, A. (1986). Claiming our destiny. (In two parts). *RID Views*. October:12 and November:3–4.

Working paper on access to justice for Deaf people
Maureen Reed, Graham H. Turner and Caroline Taylor

Introduction

16 March, Leeds (*Me, I'm Afraid of Virginia Woolf*). More filming in the Town Hall, this time in a corridor which leads from the cells. Two men are led by in handcuffs, the father and uncle of a family, both deaf and dumb. The father had been sleeping with his children and allowed the uncle to do the same. Mother, father, uncle, all were deaf and dumb, but the children could speak and speech was the father's downfall. 'Would this be any more Life,' says Hopkins in the play, 'would this be any more Life than a middle-aged lady sitting reading in a garden?' Yes, I'm afraid it would. (Alan Bennett, *Writing Home*)

Why is this area important?

40 years ago, the last ever hanging took place in our country. People are no longer hanged for criminal offences in the UK. Our system of justice does improve. One of the improvements relates to language. There is provision in the European Convention on Human Rights (paragraph 3 of article 6) for anyone charged with a criminal offence to be "informed properly, in a language which he understands and in detail, of the nature and cause of the accusation against him… and to have the free assistance of an interpreter if he cannot understand or speak the language used in court." A number of countries are making progress in ensuring that this article is made to apply to Deaf people.

Yet there is evidence, even when interpreters are present, that members of the Deaf community are still denied full access to the legal system, and therefore full access to justice. The courts are not sufficiently aware of the nature of signed language and Deaf culture and the particular circumstances of the Deaf community. Even where interpreters are available, the absence of research into bilingual BSL/English courtroom interactions means that there may be little understanding of

Not previously published.

the complex demands of interpreting within court proceedings. This paper reports on a project focussing on these matters.

What is the project called and what are its aims?

The project is called 'Access to Justice for Deaf People in the Bilingual, Bimodal Courtroom'. The aims are:
1 The gathering and collating of evidence relating to the experiences of Deaf people and interpreters in the courts.
2 The observation, recording and analysis of courtroom interactions.
3 The promotion of outcomes that will help to inform training developments and policy decisions aimed at giving Deaf people full access to justice.

Cultures and communities
Police behaviour clashing with Deaf culture

When a Deaf person gently bangs on a table, it is done to get the attention of another person. However, when a Deaf person bangs on the table—perhaps to get the interpreter's attention—during a police interview, this may be taken as a strongly aggressive signal by the police officers. On the other hand, if a police officer bangs on the table to push home a point, the Deaf person—our interview data suggest—may feel forcibly accused of committing a crime. From a Deaf perspective, such behaviour from a police officer 'translates' as meaning "We know you did it, full stop, no argument".

Interpreter arrives—Deaf person talks unguardedly

One interpreter illustrated this from his/her point of view. "The danger is, Deaf people have this urge to tell somebody! Because everyone else is telling their story and they haven't got any opportunity to tell somebody. Suddenly you're there and you can communicate with them and they want to tell you. Totally unaware of what they're doing... The danger is Deaf people because... Particularly if there are hearing people involved in the incident, they're going to see all those hearing people going up to the policeman, telling him their side of the story, the police arrive, people come up to them, and the Deaf person's saying 'I want to tell you, I want to tell you my side', and they're told 'No, wait, wait,

wait.' Talking to all these hearing people and they're telling their side of the story and an hour and a half later, this interpreter arrives who they can communicate with, they can get their side across and you're having to say 'Whoa, tell me Monday morning'."

Impressions non-signers build up of Deaf people

The crucial point about this whole area is that these are matters that permeate throughout all elements of court experiences for Deaf people, in a way that is rarely, if ever, recognised. The problem is that it runs so deep and intersects with so much that the court takes for granted. An interpreter made this point in interview: "A hearing person [defendant or witness] looks around, and they may or may not be paying attention. (A Deaf person) looks around, and the whole court knows he's not aware of what's going on. And that's *not* fair." In a courtroom, a place where we know impressions are vital, what impression will the jury get of a person who shows themself to be unconcerned about or uninterested in the proceedings?

Small examples of behaviour that will build up to affect the court's impression of the Deaf person include: the Deaf witness who belched, twice, covering his/her mouth but unfortunately still quite close to the microphone in the witness box (a microphone placed uncomfortably close in what may well have felt like a situation all too reminiscent of speech training at school): the Deaf witness who arrived in the witness box and immediately informed the court that a break would soon be needed as he/she "was diabetic, and would need some food, a chicken sandwich would be fine, or a pie, something like that": the Deaf witness who signed across the court to the clerk that he/she should "maybe get a Stenographer or typist" so that he/she wouldn't need to write everything down in longhand (the clerk's face was thunderous as he/she icily responded by saying to the interpreter "maybe you could ask the witness just to respond to the question"): the Deaf witness—a man—who answered the questions in BSL accompanied by an incomprehensible, high-pitched, whine-like vocalisation of which he appeared entirely unaware.

One tiny moment of courtroom interaction can be so influential in leading those present to one perception or another of witnesses and defendants. Barristers know this very well, and they develop great skill in using this knowledge. Let's give an example. One barrister made the following suggestion to a witness in discussion of damage done to a Deaf person's house: "[The defendant] had, as [the house-holder] would probably put it, 'weed' on the chair downstairs". It looks so trivial and innocuous, does it not? But think for a minute. This "weed" was not used by an interpreter prior to this suggestion from the barrister. It was uttered in such a manner as to show the barrister's uncomfortable feelings at having to speak like this in court. So why did the barrister use it? It is an informal word that English-speakers are likely to associate with naivety and childhood. It is not the kind of word one would expect in court: 'urinated', probably, 'peed' perhaps (from a witness) or 'pissed' (from a witness being ostentatiously disrespectful). Yet the barrister—who was representing the Deaf house-holder—not only chose it, but specifically attributed his/her choice to the claim that the Deaf person would 'probably' have used that word.

On what basis, one wonders, does the barrister reach this conclusion? Does it not tell us something quite specific about the way he/she views this Deaf person or wants the court to view him/her—as being perhaps naive, perhaps childish, ignorant of the language expected in a court of law, or too poorly-educated to have the necessary vocabulary beyond this 'easy' word, or both? On what would these views be founded? And, perhaps most significantly of all, what does it tell us that the barrister showed no compunction in presuming to communicate these assumptions to the court? Perhaps that they were assumptions that the other English-speakers present would find plausible or could be expected to share?

False sense of security when Deaf people seem satisfied

In those situations where interpreters are provided, it is not necessarily the case that Deaf people will be asked whether they are satisfied with the interpreting provision. Sometimes the courts or police do ask—but we would wish to note that this process is not as straightforward as people would like to believe.

In the first place, a Deaf person who declares himself/herself satisfied with the interpretation is ill-informed for the making of such judgments. After all, the Deaf person may understand the interpreter, but the interpreter's signing may bear little relation to the original spoken message. Likewise, the Deaf person may understand the interpreter, but the interpreter may understand the Deaf person much less fully and therefore be reporting back to the court the contents of the Deaf person's comments with only partial accuracy. The Deaf person is simply not in a position to know. We observed one case in which two interpreters were operating on behalf of the court: the Deaf defendant in question would not accept one of the two interpreters, having seen transcripts of some of that interpreter's earlier work on the case. But, in fact, we were able to ascertain in the course of our research at this trial that the other interpreter also produced language that the Deaf person would have been entitled to consider questionable as appropriate interpretation. Having no transcript, however, of what this interpreter was saying, the Deaf person could not know what was being put before the court in his/her name.

Secondly, a number of incidents have been described to us of Deaf people—including children—being asked by the court through an interpreter if they are happy with that very interpreter. Faced directly with the person in question, who may well be known to them, it would take an extraordinarily strong-minded person to be bold enough to declare dissatisfaction. Many more people would meekly raise no objections.

Thirdly, it is rare that the Deaf person, asked to declare satisfaction with the interpreting, would know what the alternative might be. If the present interpreter is unsatisfactory, the next one may even more so—or, worse still, the alternative may turn out to be that no interpreter is provided at all.

From a Deaf perspective, one could well take the view that checking the Deaf person's satisfaction with the interpreter is a somewhat hollow or cosmetic exercise designed to meet the needs of a rulebook rather than of real people.

From our interviews, too, we have a sense of Deaf people and interpreters not quite knowing when one or other of them should seek clarification. One interpreter recounted a problem to do with the spatial layout of a scene-of-crime: "One of the opening things was to introduce a diagram of the actual plan of the house… It was interesting that it wasn't until the third morning when someone was giving evidence that it actually twigged that they were actually standing the other way around. From the word go, I'd always assumed that (the defendant) had been in the doorway… It wasn't until the Wednesday morning that I realised I'd got them all the wrong way around. Again this… is that crucial information I should have known before I actually started? I don't know. As I say, [the defendant] didn't correct me, s/he could have done. So again, does that mean s/he was understanding?"

In another interview, one interpreter spoke of the common experience that Deaf people will not indicate their lack of understanding: "Deaf people usually don't 'remain silent', just give it out like that, usually I find, generally speaking, deaf people are very honest and open, you know, and just straight, direct, to the point… If they don't understand when their rights are said to them, and they don't fully understand and they look at me and I know they won't say 'no, they don't understand', they usually nod."

Use of audist terminology

Many instances have come up in our records when court officers and legal professionals have given accidental hints that they have some—charitably, let's say—'old-fashioned' views about Deaf people. Whilst the court likes to see the interpreter as its own agent, this does not prevent it being common that one should hear utterances such as "Because we have [a Deaf defendant] who needs the services of a sign interpreter…" Who needs the interpreter? Is this trivial quibbling, or is it indicative of a prevailing view about Deaf people as being the 'needy' ones in this interaction?

One magistrate in interview commented that the mental capacity of Deaf people was, "of course", not assured. This magistrate had overheard comments from the public gallery supporting this opinion, and declared that he/she had consequently dealt with the interpreting "leniently". In other words, he/she had not queried any issues causing puzzlement during interpreted parts of testimony, because he/she simply put these down to the allegedly inferior mental capacity of Deaf persons. Other observations of court proceedings periodically throw up utterances such as (from a barrister) "… for reasons of which you are unaware, since you are, unfortunately, deaf…"; the oft-heard phrase "deaf and dumb"; reference to a Deaf witness as "a profoundly deaf" (with the usual word "person" conspicuous by its absence).

What should we make of these? The two most likely interpretations seem to be (a) the speakers really do have these impressions about Deaf people and the kind of behaviour that is appropriate with respect to Deaf people or (b) they consider it to be efficacious, when before the court, to let it appear that they view Deaf people in these ways. Why would they do so? Only if they believed that judges, magistrates and juries would be more sympathetic to their case if they treated Deaf people in these 'old-fashioned' ways.

Psychiatric and educational reports on Deaf people: Fitness to plead issues

There is on this issue a lack of recognition of Deaf experts. Why? When a hearing psychologist is called, the first thing that is established is that he/she has a list of qualifications and credentials as long as your arm. This is done to impress the jury: 'he/she is eminently qualified, so what he/she says will be true'. We observed one hearing expert stepping into the witness box with the barrister telling the jury that he/she "is able to explain the probable reactions of Deaf people". This claim begs so many questions it is not true!

Knowing your rights
Lack of information to the Deaf person in the absence of interpreter

Our research has uncovered instances in which Deaf people have been kept waiting for many hours before an interpreter's services have been secured. During this time, there is often an almost total lack of information to the Deaf person about why he/she is required. At least one instance has been reported to us in which the police have called a Deaf person in for questioning long after the crime occurred and, even though the interview was planned and booked in advance, still left the Deaf person sitting for several hours until an interpreter arrived.

Another Deaf interviewee recounted being asked to write answers to the police officer's questions, even though he/she could not write well. Only much later in the court did the Deaf person discover that his/her very personal and poorly-expressed comments and questions to the police officer were in fact being used as exhibits in a major trial.

Whilst there have been some local initiatives, supported by police forces, to develop information on videotape which can be shown to Deaf people encountering legal situations, these have not yet been expanded to a national scale. From a Deaf perspective, the result can be that any visit to a court or police station is full of anxiety, frustration and incomprehension.

Lack of information about Deaf person's rights with regard to interpreting

Most Deaf people who come into contact with the law have no idea what their rights are. A typical comment relates to the sudden appearance of an interpreter at the police station: "I don't know where they came from. The police chose one for me… How they chose them I don't know."

Also in our interviews, we have found evidence of Deaf people being given specific, but entirely mistaken, instructions about the use of interpreters. One Deaf person in interview told us that he/she was told that he/she was not allowed to ask for clarification of the interpreter's signing in court. "In the police station there was a lot of repetition, and asking for clarification. In the Crown court, they don't do that. They ask you questions, then you answer them and sit down. That's that."

It is quite clear from our interviews that Deaf people are not the only ones who are confused about what their rights are in the legal context. Here's one interpreting interviewee: "Basically it was about lawyers going into long dissertations about the law and arguing with a […] judge about this or that case that they were quoting as precedent. During this I was getting into a bit of a sweat, if you like, over getting it out right […] I was finding it quite stressful. The Deaf person was getting a glazed look in his eye, which I don't think was to do with him not understanding what I was communicating to him, but which was to do with the fact that we were into the third or fourth hour of legal argument. The solicitor was saying to me 'Don't worry, you don't need to interpret this, he won't understand it anyway, its only legal argument.' To this my immediate response, off the top of my head, was 'Well, he's got a right not to understand'. That's actually quite important." This tells us that some interpreters, at least, think that Deaf people have a right to have access to everything going on in the legal situation, whether they understand it or not (just like hearing people).

On the other hand, we also have evidence from other interpreters of quite different circumstances. "A number of things that have happened this week have made me sort of query whether [the defendant] was actually, I don't know how to say it, entitled to know everything that was going on in Court. There were a number of issues that have arisen, for example the barrister saying 'ah well, when I give my summing up... I think it will be impossible to interpret. I don't think I'll have you interpreting my summing up, to [the defendant].' So when me and [the defence interpreter] challenged that he said 'well, quite often the prisoner in the dock could be down in the cells, could be taken out of court, and the trial continues without them.' So it's actually not that relevant that [the defendant] follows everything that's going on... Which made me think, well, the only important people who've got to understand what's going on in that court are the jury. They've got to fully understand..." Yet this is, in fact, quite contrary to the European Convention on Human Rights that we quoted at the beginning.

We have even gathered evidence of interpreters using the argument that the Deaf defendant must have had months' worth of discussion and exploration about the facts of the case, and therefore when it comes to Court, the interpreter doesn't need to be too careful. The Deaf person has, said one interpreter, seen a great deal of the evidence in the run-up to the trial, and is very familiar with that evidence. So the pressure on the interpreter to achieve accuracy is less, said this interpreter, because the Deaf person knows the material well enough to 'fill in the blanks' in the interpreter's rendition.

Lack of witness support for Deaf people

Whilst the courts have taken some steps in recent times to make the process of appearing as a witness less daunting, these steps have not made the experience any the less alarming for Deaf people. A leaflet is sent to witnesses when they are summoned to appear—but it is not available in BSL. A telephone helpline is open to those needing 'witness support'—but there is no text-telephone number. From a Deaf perspective, this does nothing to open up the legal system to the full participation of Deaf persons.

Unawareness among Deaf witnesses of the way they must behave

Not only is this an issue, but it is one that can have immediately unwelcome consequences for Deaf people. In one case that we observed, the application for bail by a Deaf defendant was refused because it was said to be "a feature of this case" that Deaf people were communicating with each other across the court when they should not do so. The court clearly felt that this demonstrated that Deaf people do not appreciate and cannot be trusted to conform to the legal rules relating to communication between different parties involved in a case, 'interference with witnesses', et cetera.

And indeed it has been our observation that a number of Deaf people are not fully aware of these rules. In a case where there are several Deaf witnesses, these people are not allowed to discuss the case together whilst the court is hearing the evidence—that means at any time from day one of the case until after the verdict. The law deals sharply with people who do not observe those rules. Yet we have watched Deaf people flaunting the rules, and even doing so right outside the courtroom, either unaware that they are in breach of the law, or banking—it seems—on the fact that the court officers do not understand their sign language and assuming that they will get away with it. Which is exactly what happens: we have equally seen and heard legal professionals (eg police personnel) asking each other what to do when they witness suspicious-looking conversations between Deaf people who should not be talking to each other—and coming to the conclusion that they could do nothing.

One Deaf prosecution witness in a case we observed had visited the Deaf defendant in prison. "Were you not aware," asked a defence barrister, "that this was an unwise thing to do? Had the prosecution not told you that this was not wise?" The witness replied: "No-one told me I wasn't allowed to go." It is reasonable to assume that he/she was in fact told: it is also quite possible that he/she was not told in such a way that the position was made entirely clear. The legal position is that the witness should understand that communication with defendants is not permitted: but this cannot be enforced—all that can be enforced is that the witness be told and be required to state that he/she does understand. Realistically, we know that it is entirely plausible that the police told the Deaf witness, and asked whether it was understood, and that the witness—wanting to go home, tired of attempting to understand and make himself/herself understood through an interpreter, and well aware of what the result might be if he/she answered 'no'—simply nodded. Probably no further checks would have been made.

We would be foolish not to recognise, of course, that Deaf people may sometimes not be unaware of the court's culture, but simply using the fact that they are Deaf (and that, consequently, the court officers have difficulty in communicating with them) as a smokescreen for indulging in what they know to be improper behaviour. Some Deaf people know very well how to 'play the system' when it suits them. Whichever is the truth in any particular circumstance, the fact is that it is the presence and nature of signed language within the legal context that allows problems to arise.

Isolation of Deaf prisoners

Given that there are a relatively small number of Deaf people held in prison or on remand in the UK, it is most unlikely that any Deaf individual will be placed with others who can communicate with him/her in a signed language. Few prison staff have been trained in BSL, either. The result, from a Deaf perspective, is that once imprisoned, and even while awaiting trial, the Deaf person is left to feel extraordinarily isolated and lonely: as one Deaf interviewee explained, "I was isolated. I couldn't believe I was in prison. They put me in the wrong place. I felt I was not one of them. They put me in a special green uniform to mark me out: but I was still a human being, only Deaf… I was so alone—no-one to talk to. It's so lonely. I was alone in a big world… There were times when people spoke down to me—I had to tell them I was Deaf. Once they know that, they don't want to bother with you. In fact they don't want to know you."

We are also aware from our observations that Deaf people held on remand may be subjected to some threatening and violent treatment from other prisoners, and—allegedly—from prison staff. We have witnessed defendants complaining to the courts of being beaten up whilst on remand, to the extent that they were relieved to arrive at the court each day for the gruelling marathon of an interpreted trial, just because it allowed them a break from prison. What effect does the remand period have, one wonders, on defendants once the case comes up in court? Can it influence what they say, what they don't say, the way they say it? Are such influences different, perhaps magnified, for Deaf defendants?

Professionalism and good practice
Ill-prepared interpreter/nervous interpreter

Two kinds of nervousness have emerged from our interviews with interpreters. The obvious kind is this: "It scared the hell out of me, because I didn't know how the system worked. I didn't know who was who, what was where, what the intentions behind it were, what was the role of the judge... , you know, why there were three judges sitting there one day and only one the next day."

The less obvious kind is this: "I had worked in a hostel for ex-prisoners, which quite frequently involved going to court. I did a sort of training course before I did that, which involved work with the probation service, have been in prisons a lot, visiting people, before I got involved in what I do now. So in a sense the courtroom held less fear for me than the business of being a sign language interpreter did. So, if you like, I came into it from a different angle. I think some interpreters—very understandably—are very wary, even frightened, of the courtroom: of the ethos, the whole environment of the court situation, whilst being confident with their sign language. I feel I came in from the other direction. The courts didn't pose too much of a threat for me; sign language did, and still does."

The nervousness need not be manifested during the interpreting process. Interpreters are sometimes called to give evidence about the interpreting they provided at earlier stages in the case (eg in the police station). "I had three questions prior to that that (sic) each required a 'yes' from me, and I said 'yes... yes... yes...'. And, you know—well, I don't know if you know—but when you, when you're tense and obviously when you start going through a series of 'yeses', you say 'yes' to the next one even though it could be a 'no'. And I stood there and I saw [the defence interpreter] say, to the barrister, 'that's not quite right'. Because there is a past, you know, when they said, you know, 'is there only a present tense in sign language', and I said 'yes'! At least someone was there, and I was so appreciative of that."

Is the interpreter qualified?

One unqualified interpreter—who does accept legal work even though he/she is not comfortable about the appropriateness of doing so—brought to our attention one perspective on the issue of the necessity of being qualified that highlights the moral dilemma that one can be faced with: "Here, there seems to be quite a lot of involvement by the deaf turning to criminal activities or they do find themselves in car crashes or whatever, you know. And I think I have every sympathy, especially for those who find themselves in accidents, you know and things like that. There's enough trauma and I do take a very subjective view on their situation and so therefore I respond subjectively [i.e. by accepting legal interpreting asignments] and not at all as professionally as some may like. But then again, what is professional, you know?" It is important to examine all sides of this conundrum carefully.

Other interpreters fall back upon the argument that, since they have never received any *complaints* about their services in legal settings, they see no reason not to continue. Think about this for a second. We have already argued that the court may get a false sense of security about the Deaf people's opinion of the interpreting, not least because many Deaf people have spent a lifetime being fed the clear impression that their views are not as valid or valuable as those of hearing people. But are the hearing people present able to judge the quality of the interpreting? The Clerk of one court to whom we spoke said that he/she had found the BSL/English interpreting there (mostly done by an unqualified interpreter) much better than the spoken language interpreting he/she'd experienced. What does that prove? It may only serve to confirm how bad the spoken language interpreting is! The BSL/English interpreter, the Clerk said, was "highly respected", since he/she had letters of recommendation from other courts—but then, how would those other courts have been able to judge the interpreter's skills? "It is better," said the Clerk, "when the interpreter is a native speaker of the court's language." Is that really true? If he/she is a native user of the court's language, then he/she is correspondingly less likely to be a native user of the non-English speaker's language.

These, then, indicate some of the ways that a court officer reaches a conclusion about the quality of the interpreting provision. Is this satisfactory? Does it reassure us that the 'lack-of-complaints' argument from interpreters is well-founded? No.

Interpreters who don't admit to their limitations

"It worries me," said one interpreter interviewee, "because I know which, which area I can't function in as an interpreter in certain situations and I know where I can say 'no'. I'm still meeting interpreters now who don't know that they can say 'no'. And if there's one thing I learnt from my training courses it's to say 'no' and assertive skills. There are interpreters still with no assertiveness skills." This interpreter ascribed the fact that some interpreters sometimes appear to behave in a way that is unrealistic with respect to their own limitations to the fact that they lack assertiveness skills. But this is not the only possible explanation, though it is doubtless part of the picture.

As one experienced interpreter put it in interview: "In courts, in an ideal world, we would have interpreters who would over the years become specialists or particularly skilled in particular areas of activity. But what is happening at the moment, I think, is that interpreters who are self-aware enough to be worried about the courtroom situation and the legal consequences of their actions, those are the very interpreters who would probably do a better job in the court. The ones who are left are often untrained and are going into courts, doing the work, because they somehow have not seen the reason for this fear [...] the people who probably would be better at the job are not doing it; and the vacuum created is being filled by people who are not competent. That is worrying me a great deal."

It is seldom noted in public—but ought not to be hidden—that interpreters can be handsomely paid for undertaking court work. It would be most surprising if this were not a factor in their decisions about accepting or refusing court work. Although the guidelines drawn up between the Association of Sign Language Interpreters, the British Deaf Association and the Crown Prosecution Service do not recommend it, we have learned that interpreters may be paid £45 or more per hour for this work, even when they are one of two or more working in the court. One interpreter, in interview, jokingly noted that a number of frequent offenders were—in effect—the providers of useful contributions to his/her livelihood: "Certainly, thinking of certain people, if any of these guys actually ever turned over a new leaf, my income would come right down!"

Interpreters who join in arranging the legal case

We have both observed and been informed in interviews of situations where an interpreter has been hired to work within a defence team—interpreting during consultations between Deaf client and solicitor, and so on—and has, over time, arrived at a situation where (perhaps entirely without realising it) his/her services are in fact being used with a much wider remit than straightforward interpreting. Interpreters get asked to advise defence and prosecution teams about language issues; about the nature of the Deaf community: about Deaf culture; about educational and psychiatric aspects of Deaf people's lives, and so forth. Do they get involved? It must depend in part on the capacity in which they are engaged. Beyond that, are they qualified for such work? Are they giving accurate answers? (Legal professionals tend to take the view, it appears, that the interpreter is 'the expert' about such Deaf- and sign language-related matters.) Is it legally wise to get involved in this way? Are there moral or professional reasons not to do so, or, on the contrary, are there moral or professional reasons for *taking* such a role?

To give one example of the kind of issue that has arisen in the course of this project: one interpreter interviewee said, "Yeah, one instance I had to explain. Yeah, hearing child, deaf parents. Again, solicitor couldn't understand why the child was aggressive and defensive of his parents who was, were victimised by a neighbour. And the child was in court, youth court, for using threatening behaviour and I had to explain to the solicitor who was questioning the lad at the time, you know, what it's like to be a child of deaf parents... And he didn't fully understand that until I'd explained to him that the lad couldn't articulate it. So when we went into court actually the solicitor had that as ammunition… [T]his kid could not articulate it, he'd never been in court before, you know, not had a history of this, the parents were desperate with him, you know, and the solicitor was, could not grasp it, he just was not grasping it. I then felt, well, I'll be blowed, I'll just say. And I signed, I said 'do you mind if I just explain a little bit of what it's like?' so I explained to the solicitor."

Interpreters' egos

One interpreting interviewee captured the experience of, in effect, having one's ego built up by repeated demonstrations by others of their dependence on you as interpreter: "I'm not a masochist but I have a passion for crisis situations. I mean I will jump in where angels fear to tread, because I suppose that's my culture. You know, get in there first, you know. As an interpreter I've worked with the police where I've actually had to go into situations first, with them behind me, you know. It's like my fear factor is [immeasurably low], you know? I think as a child of deaf parents you're put in situations where your confidence, you know, is quite high. Your confidence becomes established early on because you can talk to any stranger, you know, and you don't care what they think about you…"

Another interpreter put it most succinctly: "You have to have an ego the size of the Eiffel Tower to be an interpreter, don't you?"

Court relentless and exhausting

From a Deaf perspective, the strain of comprehending the formal and somewhat stilted interaction of the court through an interpreter can be enormous. Even Deaf people with a good knowledge of English complain about having to 'translate in one's head'. One Deaf interviewee put this very clearly: "It was like something out of a book. But with a book, you have some control. You can shut the book and put it away, but this went on and on… I couldn't take everything in at that speed—I needed time to make sense of it".

One interpreter commented on the relentlessness from his/her point of view, saying that he/she would continue interpreting until "completely shattered". But the question is not and should not be "Can the interpreter continue?" but "Is the interpreter making sense?"

Problems with the same Interpreter working in the police station and in the court

Perhaps Deaf people should be asked the following question: Would you rather wait in a police cell or on remand in prison until an appropriate 'clean' interpreter arrives; or would you prefer to risk a 'contaminated' interpreter in the hope of getting off and out quickly? And if it depends: on what? On whether you're really guilty or not? On the seriousness of the charge? How serious is serious enough to wait, then?

This same argument has successfully been used by groups campaigning in relation to other minority languages in the UK for Home Office funding for interpreter training courses. Why not for BSL? What are we waiting for?

Problems with the overuse of a particular Interpreter for police/court work

In one quite stunning instance, we watched a perfect demonstration of why it can be problematic to have the same interpreter working on any two interviews within a case. This example is also bound up tightly with the problems caused by the uncommon use of a visual-gestural language in this environment.

The actual exchange in question was deceptively simple. We observed it in court during the reading out before the jury of parts of a police station interview, involving a Deaf suspect. Not being permitted access to the transcripts from the court, we are unable to quote this example verbatim. The following exchange is a replication.
Police officer: 'Were you involved in the assault at all?'
Suspect: 'I didn't kick anyone.'
Police officer: 'Who said anything about kicking? I haven't mentioned kicking. How do you know there was any kicking if you weren't involved?'

It is easy to imagine the police officer's feelings at this point. He/she has apparently trapped the suspect into revealing that he/she does know more about the incident in question than has previously been admitted. But let us tease this apart a little. It appears from the police transcript of the interview—i.e. the account that's on paper and stands as the record of the exchange, where all and only what the Deaf person signed is uttered by the interpreter—that the Deaf person has introduced the notion of 'kicking'. Is this in fact the case?

What the interpreter was faced with, as the 'raw material' from which to construct the signed question, was the English word 'assault'. The Collins *Cobuild* dictionary says: "An assault on a person is a physical attack on them which is considered to be a crime." To convey this in a visual-gestural language is not at all straightforward, since there is no visual hook upon which to give shape to the nature of the action. There is no wholly appropriate abstract sign in BSL with which to relay the notion of 'assault' in this context. So what does the interpreter do? Quite properly (at one level), produces a sign which he/she knows to be, in fact, appropriate to the circumstances in question.

In this instance, we suggest, it is likely that the above is exactly what has happened. The interpreter had previously been engaged to provide interpreting at the police interviewing of at least one other witness/suspect in the case. The interpreter consequently knew that a significant part of the assault had consisted of kicking. The choice of sign to correspond to the word 'assault' was therefore, in part or whole, reflective of this action of kicking.

Reconstructing—forensically, as it were—the exchange that we suppose to have taken place from the Deaf person's perspective, then, the question that was posed to him/her was not "Were you involved in the assault?" but "Were you involved in the kicking?" In this context, the fact that he/she answered "I didn't kick anyone" is not in the least surprising or incriminating. And yet the legal record would have us—and the jury—believe that it certainly was so.

Nature of signed language
Lack of consideration given to the question of what it means to use a visual-gestural language

Like other members of the general public, people who work in courts can be unaware of the nature of signed languages. 'Deaf people look stupid or aggressive when they sign; it is not really language anyway; it is just broken English'—many of these are quite typical comments of the kind often heard from members of the public. "They could speak if they understood the concept of language," said one prosecution barrister in court.

"It is perfectly obvious," said another barrister in court, "that interpreting language into sign language is not and cannot be as exact a science as interpreting from one language into another." This suggests a double ignorance. Firstly, no kind of interpreting is an 'exact science', although the courts like to pretend that it is. And secondly, signed languages are one set of human languages, not—as this legal professional seemed to believe—something quite different to the things he recognised as 'language'.

Questions asked to witnesses sometimes reveal the questioner's lack of thought or knowledge about the nature of signed language. "How good or bad is sign language at communicating explanations of events that have taken place?" asked one barrister in court. If this were a question asked about a spoken language—German, for instance—these same professional people would have no hesitation in recognising it as absurd.

Another barrister was observed trying to find out from a Deaf witness how a Deaf defendant knew something. The barrister asked: "You discussed it with your friend, did you? Was the defendant in the same room?" What would this prove? Deaf people can very easily be in the same room, but not know what others are discussing, because one has to be looking at a visual-gestural conversation in order to understand it.

This point about the need to focus one's eyegaze in order to follow signed communication has relevance in other ways, too. When the subject of Deaf jurors comes up, one typical part of the reasoning as to why Deaf jurors couldn't do an adequate job is that, since they would need to be watching the interpreter, they wouldn't be able to see the demeanor and behaviour of other people present (witnesses, defendant, et cetera). If this is true, then the court should also recognise that Deaf witnesses and defendants are themselves disadvantaged because, whilst concentrating on the interpreter, they cannot keep themselves appraised of the reactions and responses of everyone else in the room (the judge, the jurors, the witnesses, et cetera). Even when a Deaf witness, let's say, is being questioned, he/she cannot sensibly look around the courtroom in between questions, since he/she must keep watching the interpreter in order to be assured of missing no part of the next question.

From a Deaf perspective, such examples as these certainly do not inspire confidence in the legal system and in professionals' awareness of Deaf people's lives, languages and cultures.

Lack of plain English in the legal system at the best of times

It should not be forgotten that the choice of dense and formal rhetorical style in the legal context—especially in written texts—stands as a hugely complicating factor for all laypersons in the courts. This is true too of interpreters and of the Deaf people whose access to the legal material is dependent on the interpreter finding ways to deal with such density in order to convey meaning accurately.

To give one example, here is the wording of the legal definition of the grounds of a defence of diminished responsibility pertaining to a murder charge: "Where a person kills or is party to the killing of another, he shall not be convicted of murder if he was suffering from such abnormality of mind (whether arising from a condition of arrested or retarded development of mind or any inherent causes or induced by disease or injury) as substantially impaired his mental responsibility for his acts or omissions in doing or being a party to the killing."

This is not easy material for a native speaker to understand, let alone to translate.

No privacy for Deaf defendants to give instructions to their representatives in court

Hearing defendants are able to make comments to their own representatives during the trial by writing notes or whispering to them. Even the literate Deaf defendant has difficulty because he/she cannot readily write a note and watch the interpreter at the same time. Deaf defendants using a signed language have much greater difficulty in keeping these comments hidden. If they privately want to remind their counsel of some crucial bit of evidence, how can they do this in open court without others being able to see it? We observed one Deaf defendant signing "That's a lie!" to his/her representative. The Deaf witness saw this, and immediately signed "It is not a lie!" across the courtroom in direct response. An argument broke out. In the end, the witness was rebuked by the court. From a Deaf perspective, this is just another small instance in which the whole experience of a trial is different for a Deaf person than for a hearing person—yet both are supposed to be equal in the eyes of the law.

One interpreter in interview made clear just how much of such commentary can be visible to others present in the court: "It was every now and again, particularly when the prosecution were making their summing up. I saw [the defence interpreter] saying to him on a number of occasions 'you know, you're just going to have to accept what they've said, because they're going to say in their favour and your barrister's going to say...' and making those sort of comments that 'you're just going to have to keep calm'. But there were the odd comments, 'oh no, they've got it wrong'... 'I didn't say that, that's not how it was'."

Deaf signing from the public gallery is visible in court

Just as Deaf defendants and witnesses can see each other's signing across the court (whereas hearing people would not hear quiet speech at such a distance), so Deaf people inside the courtroom can see the signing of people in the public gallery. People are warned not to talk in the gallery, but silent signing does not disturb the court officials—who cannot understand it even if they notice it—and so is often allowed to continue. We have observed Deaf members of the public signing cruel things to each other in full view of the Deaf defendant: and we have seen Deaf people in the gallery signing comments directly to Deaf defendants and witnesses across the courtroom. From a Deaf perspective, this is further evidence that the court is simply not aware of the implications of operating simultaneously in sign and speech.

Reference to speakers, signers and viewers

There being no such thing as courts run by and for the Deaf community, it is well-nigh impossible to know what conventions are appropriate for a BSL trial. To give a small example: where is the Deaf environment in which people are formally referred to in the third person even when they are present—eg 'The witness claims that he saw the defendant...' as uttered in court where both witness and defendant are watching the interpreter referring to them?

In the absence of such an environment, and therefore lacking the conventions to apply, the interpreter can either do what English does (and thus be somewhat un-Deaf in his/her signing) or be more Deaf (i.e. refer to those present using second person forms, directly pointing to them, an effective conveyor of the propositional meaning intended) but risk (a) being somewhat over-direct and thereby potentially oppressive or (b) over-stepping the cultural mediation mark. Neither is altogether satisfactory and neither can entirely be deemed stylistically appropriate.

Cross-modality mismatches
Interpreters may not know how to deal with visuality mismatches

Part of one of our interviews illustrates this point.
Q: 'There was a question that was actually put at one stage, 'did you hit her?'... What did you do then? You've got to decide what sort of hit it was?...'
A: 'I gave him the choice of three in fact.'
Q: 'You were actually asked?'
A: 'I said 'did you hit (demonstrates), hit (demonstrates differently), slap?' I had to give him the choice of the three. His reply was (demonstrates) and then when he got into the witness box he expanded on that.'
Q: 'Yes.'
A: 'So you give him the choice of all the variations on "hit".'
We wonder whether there are three items of BSL vocabulary which constitute "all the variations on hit"?

Visual language needs visual contextualisation

In the courts, it is expected that witnesses will keep to the point and answer the questions in a focused way as posed. In our observations, we have come across many instances in which Deaf people have instead given longer answers where it appears they are seeking to recreate some kind of visual context for recollection and refocusing of the question in hand. To take one example:
Barrister: 'Did [the defendant] and [the two witnesses] go off somewhere?'
Witness: 'Well, we all went in, it was the first time I'd been to the flat, so I had a look around, then we all sat down to chat and drink over beers. [One of the witnesses] and [the defendant] went to the toilet for a private chat.'

190   As far as the court is concerned, this is a drifting, unfocused answer to a straightforward question, and one would expect that the impression of the Deaf witness giving this answer would be coloured by this view. However, it seems at least plausible to suggest that what is actually occurring here is that the Deaf witness is formulating a visual context for his/her recollections.

Later in the same trial, it was clear that some of the police questioning of Deaf suspects from the police station (recounted in detail from the transcripts) had jumped around referring unpredictably to one room or another, one location or another. Perhaps this is usual police questioning—one could imagine that it may be a deliberate tactic to put the suspect off-guard and attempt to prise out truthful answers. Perhaps, alternatively, hearing people find this much less confusing because their mental models for responding do not have their foundations in vision in the same way. Take a (hypothetical) sequence of questions like:

1   Why did you go upstairs?
    (I went to look for money)
2   Did you leave the back door open?
    (Yes, because John might want to come in)
3   But you told us that he had run off to look for his bicycle.
    (Maybe he would find it and come back)
4   Did you look for money all over the house?
    (Yes)
5   But we only found fingerprints in the kitchen and the upstairs study.
    (I don't know why)
6   Did you disturb the contents of the bathroom cabinet?
    (No)
7   The neighbours told us they could hear you rummaging in the bathroom.
    (We never did that)
8   You left blood all over the garden path. Were you looking for a plaster in the cabinet?
    (We didn't look in the cabinet)
9   One of our officers saw John taking a bicycle from a house in the

next street.
(It was his bicycle)
10 The kids there said they'd seen John hanging around the school gates.
(He was waiting for his girlfriend)

It can be seen that the location, scale of visual space described and angle or perspective are liable to change at virtually every step of the way through this brief interchange.

For the interpreter, who has to create and sustain a visual context for each element of this interaction, and for the Deaf viewer who has to keep pace with the rapid changes of scene, this exchange takes place under considerable pressure to sustain the continuity of dialogue, keeping hold of the thread of the mental model of the scene that has been created as well as the sense of the sequentiality of questioning. There is no visual context re-established before action begins in a new scene. Unless this is managed well, the effect from the perspective of the Deaf viewer is that of unexplained visual shifting of reference so that no visual context endures to give the dialogue coherence.

If the interpreter did stop every time there was (visual) ambiguity, there'd be chaos

It is crucial to recognise the pervasive nature of visuality within the structure of BSL. It is everywhere. Structurally, it is nowhere in the English language: that is, though visual metaphor and the like may be a common feature of English-language discourse, it is not a *necessary* part of the linguistic patterning as it is in any signed language.

To reinforce this point, and to make clear how great the interpreter's dilemma is—when expected to recreate everything that is non-visually constructed in English into something that must become visual in BSL—let us give a set of examples (a tiny subset, in fact of relevant examples from a single case) of the phenomenon becoming problematical. In each case, the witnesses' comments are as voiced by the interpreter.

One
Barrister: 'And did [the defendant] show you anything?'
Witness: '[The defendant] had a crow-bar inside her… outer clothing.'

Here the interpreter pauses to search for a way of indicating the type of garment that has been indicated in BSL without over-specifying the item in question. The result is not terribly idiomatic in English.

Two

Barrister: 'What did [the defendant] do to him?'
Witness: '[The defendant] threw him back against the wall and began to… beat him with both fists.'

Again, the interpreter is searching for a way to indicate the totality of information that is included in this necessarily visual utterance of BSL, and finding that the result is over-specific for English.

Three

In one trial which we observed, an item of importance to the police enquiries was recovered having been thrown away by or on behalf of the defendant. On a number of occasions this action of "throwing away" was mentioned in the police station and court exchanges. Not once, to our knowledge, did the interpreter find out about the direction in which the throwing was done. Yet it would be impossible for the interpreter to create a visualised signing of the action without being determinate about the direction. One can only presume, then, that the interpreter either found out the direction from informal sources, or used his/her imagination to create something plausible.

Four

During the reading of a police officer's statement in court, the following was heard: "I kicked at the door four times with my left foot until the door gave way."

The Interpreter—being right-handed—had begun to sign the kicking as if with the right foot until the phrase "with my left foot" came out.

Five

Barrister: 'Why did the group split up?'
Interpreter: 'Why did three people part company from two people?' (signed)

In this instance, the questioner did not specify how many people were involved, nor into what sized groups the party split. Yet the interpreter, either knowing on the basis of the context, or making an educated guess, created the more specific question using the visual proforms of BSL.

Interpreter's choice of signs

Interpreters commonly worry—and training courses have regularly responded to the worry—about legal terminology. The language of the courts can be peppered with Latinate words, phrases and constructions (and, indeed, with items borrowed directly from Latin) and these are not easy for the interpreter—who has been asked to put everything that is said into a form that is accessible to non-English speakers—to handle.

Yet these are not by any means the only set of lexical items that cause problems, even though they attract great attention and are often given prominence. Many of the problematical signs are ones that may have an everyday general lexical function in the language which is stretched to accommodate the specific meaning attached to them in the legal context. (We are indebted to Clive Palmer who first mentioned the pervasiveness of this problem to us.)

Too many interpreters think insufficiently carefully about the appropriateness of using these general signs without, at least, further clarification. The following list identifies a number of these 'keywords'. It may be noted that many of them are difficult to translate due to the lack of visual specification needed in the English lexicon.

murder	substantial	assault
submission	liable	attack
involvement	joint enterprise	beyond reasonable doubt
cause of death	interfere	disorder
kill	crime	abnormality
the act of…	evidence	vulnerable
inference	fit to plead	severe
state of mind	provocation	intention
the law	adversity	alibi
serious	exhibit	

A final example is the word 'rape'. Again, this is not a term limited in its context of use to the courts of law. Whilst there is a single sign that is typically seen as having a one-to-one correspondence with the English word 'rape' this is an instance that illustrates the actual non-correspondence in the legal context clearly. By a legal definition, rape entails sexual penetration. The meaning of the sign commonly glossed as 'rape' in BSL carries no such entailment. We have anecdotal evidence that this mismatch has in fact been an issue in at least one legal case, where the sign was used, the gloss 'rape' was attached to it, and it was not until some way through the legal proceedings that it was discovered that—in legal terms—the alleged 'rape' was in fact no such thing.

Patterns of language differ between signed and spoken languages

One simple example gives an idea of the complexity of dealing with two very different languages at once in the courtroom. English language users in the courts tend to address their comments and questions using forms like 'Mr. Turner. would you say that…', 'That is correct, sir", "It may be, as my learned friend suggests…', 'My Lord, if you will permit…' But in BSL we don't use forms like these: you don't have to sign someone's name if you are already conversing with them. Indeed, you don't get their attention by using their name, because the nature of a visual-gestural language means that you cannot converse with them unless you already *do* have their attention. Signing their name—no matter how politely you do it—won't get their attention by itself anyway! However, in the court context, we know from other linguistic research that using forms of address as politeness markers can be a helpful strategy—other people in the court will think better of you if you do use these forms. From a Deaf perspective, does this mean that you will always be at a disadvantage if you use your native language in the usual way?

People construct accounts of events, conduct discourse and tell narratives differently in different languages

The Australian linguist Diana Eades has put a considerable amount of energy into untangling some of the implications of differential discourse patterning across languages and cultures in Australia. In particular, she has shown how Aboriginal English-speakers—whilst overtly members of the same linguistic community—use language resources, including the ever-present option of remaining silent, in some markedly different ways to other English-speakers there. Eades has applied these insights most tellingly to the legal situation in forensic linguistic studies. Her studies have uncovered disturbing evidence that members of Aboriginal communities are disadvantaged by others' perceptions of their different style of interaction.

We have some initial evidence that something similar may occur in respect of Deaf people in such settings. In particular, we suspect that being required to operate in a language that is not common to the court officials and through the medium of an interpreter may affect the evidence given. For instance, Deaf witnesses' testimony is often interrupted whilst the judge/magistrate/clerk takes written notes of the questions and answers. Whilst this may be equally true for a hearing witness, it may be the case that the stop-start process entailed is more difficult to manage for a signing person.

Secondly, one gets the impression that it is unusual in the courtroom for witnesses to give extended narrative answers to questions: in fact, these are regularly formulated to be as constraining as possible, so that the witness has only to answer 'yes' or 'no'. But there is a suggestion in our observations to date—and from our general knowledge of discourse norms in the Deaf community—that it may be more typical for Deaf people to conduct interaction with longer, more elaborately constructed accounts of events and situations. So what is the effect on such signers of being 'reined in' and required to prune their answers down to minimal responses or else to be frequently interrupted—and perhaps thrown off their train of thought—by the barrister, clerk or judge?

Interpreter's lack of control of register in BSL

We have several times observed interpreters producing a kind of signing in court that did not reflect the tone of the proceedings as they came across in English. Without video recordings (at this stage in the project, none have been made), it can be hard to pinpoint exactly what it was about a certain style on a certain occasion that struck us as anomalous. For example, we came away from one observation session agreeing that the interpreter had used a style that would have been fine for a light entertainment show of low-key humour in a provincial theatre—but was certainly not, we felt reflective of the formal language and exchanges of a higher court. As we begin to collect video recorded data from the courts in Scotland, we should be able to say more accurately what might be done to correct this apparent mismatch.

Again, we would be looking thereby to assist by providing constructive guidance to interpreters, to the benefit of the court and of Deaf people who might subsequently be better served by the language produced by that interpreter in the legal arena.

One of the reasons for this is the lack in BSL of certain markers of formality and stylistic shift. It is noticeable, for instance, that during the examination of witnesses, both defence and prosecution barristers deliver their questions in a formal but friendly style: if they are seen to be intimidating the witnesses, their cause will not be helped, whereas a friendlier approach may help them to 'draw' certain information out of the witness. One of the markers of this style is to preface questions with relatively formal, polite terms of address—"Now, Mr. Turner, would I be right in thinking… ", and so on. We have noted that such terms of address are not used in BSL. But if the interpreter does not manage to convey this sense of style and register to the viewer(s), how are they supposed to know what tone to adopt themselves?

Interpreters lack maps and plans so visual details may be wrong

This type of layout problem faced one interpreter at the end of a week in a certain trial. The interpreter, interviewed by a member of the research team, at this point said: "The placement I was using today is the result of four days' work. As we went along, I realised that, woops, we had things the wrong way round… As I got the plans, I located things more accurately." (Notice the use of the word "we" there: there was only one interpreter working at this trial, and the Deaf person knew which way round everything should be because he/she was there at the scene of the crime. 'We' has the effect of attempting to mitigate blame in a tricky situation.) It is important to recognise, of course, that the chances are that any Deaf people involved will (a) be more familiar than the interpreter with the visuo-spatial layout of the environment in question—they may well have been present on the very occasion in question—and (b) be keyed into the visual descriptions given as part of the mental modelling of context required for coherent conceptualisation within a signed framework. The result of this may well be that, whilst the interpreter perhaps does not consider visuo-spatial errors to be greatly significant—as would seem to be suggested by the casual "woops" above—the Deaf viewer is in fact on the receiving end of an extremely confused and confusing message that is hard to connect to the facts as the viewer knows them.

Another interpreter reported being called by a solicitor. The solicitor had been alarmed when hiring an interpreter to be asked for payment for the interpreter's preparation time: attendance at the scene of the crime, study of maps and plans, et cetera. The solicitor wanted to know if this was really necessary and appropriate. If the result of not having access to such material is that—surely to the detriment of the Deaf viewer's attempts to understand what is being described—the interpreter is still mislocating salient actors or features of the layout four days into the trial, then this question answers itself, does it not?

Problems with texts
Insistence upon referring back to written texts

The legal system depends very much upon written transcripts as records of what the police or the courts have been told. Deaf people, along with speakers of foreign languages, are put at a disadvantage by this. The 1983 European Court of Human Rights judgment in the Kamasinski case—in which a citizen of the USA imprisoned in Austria claimed breaches of human rights legislation with regard to interpreting—said that, in principle, the human right to interpreting provision extends beyond the courtroom to include written statements and documents needed by the defendant in putting a case before the court. In practice, we have observed numerous occasions when Deaf people are disadvantaged by their lack of access to written materials. This is a key area of difficulty.

Probably the most striking illustration in our data is as follows. When a Deaf person is questioned by police, a written script is made of the conversation, and the Deaf person is required to sign the script to show that it is an accurate record. Since many Deaf people cannot read the script well, it is common practice for the interpreter to sign the full script back to the Deaf person. If he/she is satisfied, then he/she signs the paper. At one point in a trial that we observed, the following exchange took place. A Deaf witness is being asked to consider the written script from his/her police interview which is placed before him/her.

Barrister: 'Can you read English?'
Deaf witness: 'No.'
Barrister: 'Not at all?'
Deaf witness: 'Nothing at all.'
(The judge checks that the correct procedure was followed in the police station. It was.)
Barrister: 'Well, this is your words to the police... Will you take it from me that in August 1994 you said...'

Let us look at this again. The words that are now put before the court are in no sense a record of exactly what the Deaf person actually signed in August 1994, yet the court operates on the basis that they are the same in every relevant detail. The Deaf witness is in fact being asked to accept (a) one interpreter's rendition of (b) a barrister's reading of (c) a police officer's written text taken from (d) another interpreter's spoken translation of (e) what that witness actually signed in the police interview room. This is not 'the same words': this is four steps removed from being 'the same words'. So when the barrister says 'Will you take it from me that you said... .?' he/she is actually asking a great deal more than the court realises.

We observed another witness on another occasion being asked to look at a written exchange he/she had had with the police when questioned in the police station without an interpreter. The witness was asked to locate on the page placed before him/her a certain line—"Is she expecting you?" The witness could not read well enough to find this line. The usher pointed it out to him/her. No Deaf person, we suggest, would be in any doubt about the sinking feeling that must have accompanied this exchange for the witness—to be 'exposed' in this way in a court of law. It should be a matter of no shame to Deaf BSL-users that their English skills are not necessarily native-like in fluency. The defence barrister questioning this Deaf witness made as much capital as possible out of what the witness had or had not written in these statements. Yet the witness could not even locate the line at which the discussion began! Does this not suggest that questions must be asked about how this witness could have been conducting a sensible written exchange in the first place? (In fact, the witness had later been interviewed via an interpreter: the police had realised that this was necessary.

But that didn't prevent the written exchange being used as important evidence upon which the witness was cross-examined at length.)

No video record is kept

'Court sign language mistake halts trial', said page 3 of a 1995 issue of the London *Daily Telegraph*. The report that followed alleged that an error by an interpreter "caused the collapse of an eight-week murder trial which had cost the taxpayer more than £1 million." The interpreter, it said, admitted the mistake and said it occurred through tiredness. But what really happened in this trial, or indeed in any other trial involving signed language? The truth is that no-one can ever know for certain once the trial is over, because no video-recording is made of any of the signing. Did the interpreter really make an error? Was it the only error? It is very hard to be sure.

In fact the legal process keeps a great deal of its records on paper at every stage, and virtually nothing is video-recorded. Police interviews are almost never video-recorded: solicitor's consultations likewise: and court proceedings in England, Wales and Northern Ireland must not be filmed by law. Without such a record, however, no Deaf person can ever check what he/she signed or what an interpreter signed, and the bilingual, bimodal court cannot keep a fully accurate record of the exchanges that took place within its four walls.

Some of the examples we could give to illustrate the dangers are very complex: here is a simple one. The defence barrister and the clerk of the court took great care during one of our visits to court, to check whether the interpreter had prefaced his/her translation with the words 'I think'. It was very important, in the context of that case, to know whether the witness was 100% sure of his story. But who actually uttered the words 'I think?' Did they come from the interpreter, indicating that he/she was not sure of the meaning of something that had been signed, or from the witness? Without a video-recording, there's no knowing.

Evidence put before the Court on paper is not straightforward for Deaf people

The court considers much of its evidence on paper rather than calling each witness in person. Even where this evidence is pictorial—e.g. photographs of the scene of the crime—courts tend to forget that Deaf people cannot look at the papers and the interpreter at once and so are disadvantaged unless extra time is allowed.

When the evidence is in the form of written texts or tables of information, Deaf people find this even harder to deal with. We know from both observation and interview that from a Deaf perspective, much of this presentation of information is oppressively reminiscent of school. Even Deaf people who have become enemies glance at each other's papers as they sit side by side in the dock, nervously checking that they have found the right page and so will not appear foolish to the court officials and legal personnel. Some pretend to read even if they understand very little.

Likewise, one Deaf defendant we saw in court was most helpfully served by his/her solicitor who found the relevant page of text for him/her in the bundle of papers presented whenever necessary. But how did this apparent dependency look to the court? Did it make the Deaf person look more or less sensible, independent, clear-headed, intelligent?

Similarly, we were told of a custody case for which, on the day of the crucial hearing, the mother arrived at court with an interpreter and her social worker as well as her legal representatives, whereas the father turned up alone and proceeded to conduct his own case. Whilst the mother appeared—we were told—in the eyes of others present, rather helpless, dependent and incapable, the father gave every impression of being supremely competent and strong.

The introduction of different signs and different stories

When there is no video-recording of the Deaf person's statement to police, any subsequent 'quotation' from that statement treads on somewhat thin ice. That is to say, if a Deaf witness is asked on oath—as he/she almost inevitably will be—to take the court once again through the details of his/her statement to the police, then it is important for that witness' credibility that the account put forward on this occasion matches, in every relevant aspect, the account originally given to the police. Any significant deviation, and the court will, at the very least, want to be given a solid explanation for the change. If none is forthcoming, then the way is open for the conclusion that the witness is guilty of obfuscation or duplicity.

Yet it must be acknowledged, surely, that it is virtually impossible for the Deaf witness to achieve consistency in this way. He/she has no BSL 'text' to recount. What is in the police statement text, in English, may be inaccessible and/or subject to interpreter error, especially if it has been signed as 'accurate' by a witness unable, in fact, to read it.

To make matters more complicated, the interpreter who (a) gave voice to the Deaf person's signed account at the police station and (b) recounted that account to the Deaf person on the basis of the police text in order that this be signed as 'accurate' (i.e. who has had two chances, at least, to introduce problems or anomalies), that interpreter is unlikely to be the same interpreter who is now going to (i) give voice to the Deaf person's court testimony and (ii) repeat passages of the statement to the Deaf witness when required to do so by the defence/prosecution barristers. So again, we see that there are multiple opportunities for slippage and modified interpretations which could lead to doubt in the minds of judges, magistrates and jurors.

To give a sense of how this might occur, just imagine the number of times in which it would be possible for the two different interpreters to use different signs or different words in presenting and representing information. In the first kind of instance, the Deaf witness may look as if they are trying to cover something up since 'you knew perfectly well what X meant when you were asked on the 13th of July 1993'. In the second, the Deaf witness may appear to be changing their story since 'On the 13th of July 1993, you told PC McGarry that the defendant was waving a broom-handle at you: now you say it was a baseball bat'.

This kind of problem can even arise within the court proceedings if there are two interpreters at work who do not—for whatever reason—manage to achieve consistent inter-interpreter choice of lexis. We have indeed seen this happen in court. The risk of worse exists, but at the very least it presents another point at which the Deaf viewer is liable to be genuinely confused by the inconsistency, since he/she will not know whether the original English utterances were equivalent to each other or not. In other words, if the Deaf person sees one sign used with the meaning 'alcohol' at one moment, and a different one the next, what can he/she conclude but that the English words uttered on these two occasions were different?

Arrangements within the courtroom
Taking of the oath

In an immaculate demonstration, at the very outset of many of the legal proceedings we have observed, of the ill-thought-through communication arrangements, even a fundamental act such as the witnesses' taking of the oath raises problems. It is important to note that these arise not through the inadequacy of anyone present, but through the court's lack of practical recognition of the nature of the communicative event about to unfold before it.

"I swear by Almighty God to tell the truth, the whole truth, and nothing but the truth": this is the wording of the most common oath in England/Wales/Northern Ireland. Most English-speakers utter this oath at the outset of their testimony, reading from a prepared card so that the actual words they utter conform to a standard, formulaic pattern.

This already presents problems. In the first place, there is no way that a signer could formally sign the oath whilst holding such a card. In the second place, there is no writing system for BSL. In the third place, there is no agreed form of wording in BSL that conventionally indicates all and only that which is indicated by the English sentence.

The result of these circumstances is typically that the Usher reads out the words from the card: the Interpreter signs them back to the witness: and the witness responds to them in such a way as to demonstrate his/her agreement to adhere to the undertaking given. The practical achievement of this interaction seems usually to require that the oath be read clause by clause, interpreted clause by clause and responded to—either by repetition or simply signing "yes" or "I agree"—clause by clause.

But this is a nonsense. The witness has not *uttered* the oath (in many instances which we have observed, the interpreter has not even uttered the oath as a 'voice-over' on his/her behalf). What the witness has communicated has been dealt with clause by clause, in such a fashion that it is utterly impossible for the signing viewer-producer to know what he/she is assenting to until he/she has finished assenting to it. That is, if the interpreter signs 'I swear by Almighty God' and the witness responds by signing 'Yes', then the perlocutionary force of the words is entirely non-existent. The witness declares that he/she 'swears' but doesn't yet know what about.

Difficulties for Deaf defendants in communicating with their own legal representatives

Unless there are a sufficient number of interpreters present, or the Deaf person's representatives can sign, the Deaf defendant may be faced with considerable difficulty in passing messages to his/her own counsel (e.g. should he/she wish to raise an objection). It is usual for hearing people to do this in writing, but many Deaf people are not able to express their views clearly in this way. One Deaf defendant shouted something out loud to his/her defence team. With great concern, they stopped the proceedings and got the court interpreter down to help them find out what objection or private comment the Deaf person wanted to make. It turned out that all the Deaf defendant had shouted was "Water!"—he/she was thirsty. This simply indicates how unprepared the court is for the interpreted use of two languages. From a Deaf perspective, the result may be at best that the Deaf person struggles to communicate with his own defence team, and at worst that the Deaf person becomes resigned to the role of passive viewer, rather than feeling that he/she has an important part to play in conducting his/her defence.

Location of the interpreter—not a Deaf choice

An exemplary vignette: when the trial begins, the interpreter is asked by the judge where he/she wishes to stand. After some thought, the interpreter asks for permission to stand alongside the judge, near to the witness box. This may help the interpreter—who can now see the witness' signing very clearly—but it makes life very difficult for the Deaf defendant who is placed on the opposite side of the room, many metres away and has to strain his/her eyes to see the interpreter clearly. The Deaf defendant is not asked where he/she wishes the interpreter to stand. From a Deaf perspective, it seems that the court considers the interpreter's needs to be more important than those of the Deaf person.

Court taking no practical steps to respond to Deaf people's views about the interpreting even when they are made known

Another vignette: the witness signs that he/she doesn't understand the interpreter and would prefer a Deaf friend to come down from the public gallery to relay interpret. The friend stands up. "No, no," says the clerk of the court, "how can we possibly accept this person as an interpreter when there are already several qualified interpreters in the room?" The court officials agree to try and continue, but to take things s-l-o-w-l-y. The friend stands up several times as apparent misunderstandings occur. The court does not allow such behaviour in the gallery. Eventually, the friend is told that he/she will be sent to the cells if this continues. From a Deaf perspective, the witness' original concerns are thereafter simply overlooked.

Reliance on court interpreters also to take instructions

In some instances, of course, there is a separate interpreter for the defence team. One court interpreter explained why this was important to him/her: "He was asking me questions. He would make comments like 'he's got it right', 'that's not right'. And that's where it's useful to have a second interpreter because as soon as somebody starts talking your eyes pick up that information, you start processing that as well as listening to what someone's saying. So it's useful to be able to say 'Tell [your defence interpreter], tell him/her… , a hearing person can call his solicitor over and say 'so and so, and so and so' and the solicitor would go across to the barrister. So it's just offering him the same sort of process that he can speak to his interpreter, the interpreter then leans across to his barrister, and says what he's said."

Is the Interpreter there for the gallery's benefit too?

One interpreter told us that he/she had on occasion actively prevented himself/herself being seen by those in the public gallery by opting to stand with back to the gallery, arguing that this would improve the interpreting. That interpreter informed us that he/she was actually verbally abused by the Deaf audience for this action, since they insisted that, as taxpayers, they had a right to have access to the court's proceedings.

This seems to be a grey area, though you wouldn't think so from the way some interpreters speak about it: "There have been BSL users in the gallery, and.., to hell with them. Sorry. That's not what I'm there for… it's incidental."

Interaction and interreting
Answers that the Deaf person is not permitted to finish

The witness begins to sign an answer and is half-way through his/her explanation when the judge says "Wait, wait, I need time to make my notes". The interpreter stops speaking when the judge speaks, and is not given a chance to finish speaking. Thus, because of the time-lag in interpreting, the Deaf person has signed things which the court does not know about. How can the Deaf person tell whether his/her interrupted answer has been relayed in full to the court? To make matters worse, when the judge says "Please continue", who begins to speak? Not the interpreter, completing his/her account of what the Deaf person had signed so far and allowing the Deaf person to finish his/her explanation, but the barrister, asking a new question! We observed one such interchange in which the judge eventually intervened:
Judge: "He keeps saying things and you continue talking."
Barrister: "Oh, I'm sorry, my lady, I didn't realise that was happening."
Judge: "Yes, well. I'm worried that you're not allowing him to speak."
From a Deaf perspective, this results in the Deaf person being prevented from telling his/her side of the story properly.

The interpreter's ability to confuse even when no actual errors occur

On many occasions, we have observed interpretation that—though one would probably not be able to identify significant errors—can only have made the Deaf person's efforts to follow the trial confusing and difficult. For instance, we observed an interpreter folding his/her hands together during pauses in the middle of spoken questions. "I didn't understand that interpreter well," signed one Deaf witness to us, "he/she was always breaking things up". From a Deaf perspective, this pose appears to indicate that the speaker has reached the end of an utterance—but what the interpreter has signed does not make sense, since the sentence has not in fact been completed. The speaker then continues, and the interpreter recommences signing.

Another—once again, deceptively simple—example reinforces both the point and the likelihood of it being relevant. A barrister said to a pathologist "You found [the defendant's] blood—as a possible source—on the trouser leg." The interpreter had to indicate one trouser-leg or the other, and opted for the right leg. The pathologist went on to describe the stain on the left leg. The interpreter went on to refer thereafter to the left leg. Of course, this instance looks fairly trivial from the point of view of a hearing person who knows that there has been an understandable and explicable inconsistency (one which is not anyway of concern to the monolingual English user). But for the Deaf person, this is just one more unnecessarily confusing example. The stain has suddenly and unaccountably migrated from right to left leg. Put yourself in that Deaf person's shoes. Perhaps you were mistaken when you thought you saw the right leg being indicated in the first place? Perhaps you were at fault for not paying proper attention? Perhaps the interpreter did change it—but why? Perhaps the interpreter accurately repeated what was said in the court, and the court personnel were confused. The Deaf person has no more likely explanation for their confusion, given the apparent satisfaction of the court, but to blame themself for lacking concentration or some such. There is no-one else to blame, apparently. No-one else seems to feel that there has been any problem. Is it likely that they are all wrong? Now multiply this small example by tens and hundreds for the times that it occurs in one way or another during a trial.

Lack of access to off-trajectory talk

Unless the interpreter is superhuman, there will be times during legal proceedings when utterances are produced—either in English or in BSL—and not interpreted to those who cannot access them directly. This may take the form of muttered exchanges between baristers, just as it may be talk that is shared between interpreter and witness (e.g. when the interpreter is asking the witness to expand upon and clarify some point).

The clerk in one trial we observed asked the interpreter to repeat something that had been said as a voice-over of the Deaf witness' account. No problem with this—except that the witness could see a question being asked and answered, but could not know what it was or why it had been asked. As soon as it was answered, the next question came from the barrister: the interpreter may or may not, in that instance, have intended to explain to the witness. The fact is that he/she did not do so. Put yourself in that witness' shoes. How do you feel? Virtually everyone in this courtroom is a member of a 'hearing society' that has historically held sway over members of your culture and has, it is often said, been responsible for some devastating oppression of people like you. How do you feel, if not, at the very least, excluded?

For the Deaf witness, perhaps the most impactful occasion for such talk is when a break is taken by the court. As the judge or magistrate leaves the room, the courtroom relaxes into informal talk and exchanges. Again, putting yourself into the Deaf person's shoes, how does this feel? What are they talking about? Fair enough, you are used to this happening: it goes on everyday of your life in all manner of environments. But here, in a court of law, is it not somehow more threatening?

The same, it has to be noted, must to an extent be true for hearing people. Police officers do not know what is discussed by interpreter and Deaf person when the tape recorder is switched off. But they must have their suspicions. What difference do these make?

Interpreter modifies the question: Deaf person gives an off-beam answer

"It is fairly typical of these (police) interviews," said one barrister to the court, "that the answers don't quite tie up with the questions, don't agree…" Here we see that the court may at times have some awareness that there can be problems in the smooth 'co-construction' of question-answer sequences—but the implications here and elsewhere remain unaddressed.

We have routinely observed slight amendments of meaning generated within the interpreter's rendition of a question/answer affecting the course of subsequent interaction. A number of these instances appeared to come about because of the interpreter's inability to divorce present utterances from those previously heard and seen. To give just one example: we watched one interpreter—who knew from earlier interaction within the case that four persons had been involved in a certain activity—produce what could be construed as a 'leading question' as a result of his/her own prior knowledge.

Barrister: 'Do you remember who went upstairs?'
Interpreter: 'Do you remember which four people went upstairs?' (signed)
Witness: 'PJ, RT, CT and.. no… wait… DL? No. I can't remember. Four. Four of them.' (signed)

A range of similar examples of what we have called 'off-beam' answers—each of which can result in nothing less than puzzlement, and rather perhaps suspicion, amongst those hearing persons listening to them—follows. In each instance, we suggest, it is probable that some slight difference in the way the question was actually signed by the interpreter may have been responsible for the 'off-beam' answer. The potential for the Deaf persons responding thus to seem evasive, foolish, confused or untrustworthy is unmistakable. The point to bear in mind is that the hearing audience and the questioner have heard one question asked, whereas what the interpreter seems actually to have posed to the Deaf person is something different. In each case, the answer given quotes the interpreter's voice-over.

1 Q: 'Did you leave the public house at about closing time?'
A: 'Yes, we went, at half past eight, to the pub. We walked. Got to the pub, had a chat, had a few drinks, I had five pints (that was the men). Kathy, I think she had Bacardi. I can't remember the name of the drink she was drinking.'
Q: 'All I would like to know is whether you left at closing time, yes or no?'
A: 'Yes.'

2 Q: 'Just want to be clear. Did all three—Sally, Gemma and Leanne—come back to Sally's house together or not?'
A: 'Went in, upstairs, in the bedroom, not me, it was Gemma. Not Gemma. Leanne opened the door, went in upstairs and to the bathroom.'

Q: 'What I'd like to know. You leave the pub. You go to Sally's house with Gemma Deans. Next time you see them, are they all together?'
A: 'Two, three, two ... three. I think one of them was missing.'

3 Q: 'Does she have a violent temper?'
A: 'She's mad, completely mad.'
Q: 'Does she have a violent temper?'
A: 'Oh yes.'
Q: 'Does she only lose her temper when she's been drinking?'
A: 'Oh she drinks doubles, pints...'
Q: 'My fault. Is it the case that she only loses her temper when she's been drinking?'
A: 'Yes, that's right.'

4 Q: 'What, if anything, did Zak say that he had done to the man?'
A: 'Geoff did, yes.'
Q: 'But what did Zak say that he had done to the man?'
A: 'I never saw that.'
Q: 'I'm asking what Zak said he had done to the man.'
A: 'Geoff and Zak did talk about it. I didn't see them. I was in the kitchen.'

Overlapping talk

It is known from other research into legal interaction that the management and production of any bits of talk that overlap—i.e. where more than one person is speaking at once—can be of significant impact in the court. For an interpreter, any instance in which two people are producing language at the same time means being forced into a position where one has to choose whose talk to represent. That is, if two people talk at once, for instance, the interpreter can't 'voice-over' both of them. He/she is forced to make a difficult choice. No convention prejudges what the interpreter ought to do at this point: he/she makes up his/her own mind in the particular context of talk. This is one of those instances where some models look good, but in practice are inadequate to cope with real talk.

Now, when an objection or similar unexpected interjection is made in court, and talk overlaps, the Deaf witness may inadvertently come out looking rude or incapable. In a particular instance from our observations, a Deaf witness was asked "Did X and Y understand each other?" An objection was raised at once: how would the witness know whether these two other people understood each other? But even as the objection was being made—hard on the heels of the question—the witness, looking visibly puzzled to see the objector suddenly rise to his/her feet, but knowing no better, began to sign an answer to the question as posed. The interpreter opted to give a spoken interpretation of the witness' comments, rather than ignoring the witness' talk and signing to him/her an interpretation of the objection being put forward. The reaction from the magistrate, the clerk and other court officers and legal representatives was immediately to frown in the direction of the witness—why was he/she continuing to talk when the question had been annulled by the objection? In point of fact, the Deaf witness did not—and indeed could not—even know that an objection had been voiced.

Here we see a canonical example of how both Deaf person and interpreter are made vulnerable by the court's lack of appreciation and practical recognition of the requirements of the bilingual, bimodal courtroom. It is an example that suggests that the primary threat to justice is not Deaf people's supposed ignorance of the law or their rights within the law, nor the alleged incompetence of interpreters working in this sector, but weaknesses in the social and linguistic environment in which legal transactions are conducted. This is not a matter for saying, censoriously, "Deaf people should learn better". It is not a matter for saying, "Interpreters should do their job more effectively". Both have acted in the best of faith towards the just outcome sought by the law. Yet the position the court puts them in can, as this kind of example highlights, be untenable.

Different interpreters means different questions

There are always dangers inherent in the process of one interpreter attempting to meet the needs of more than one consumer. One suggestion that has been put forward, with—it seems—increasing forthrightness, towards finding a resolution to such problems is that there should be one interpreter per defendant in any case featuring multiple defendants. This has been particularly firmly pushed in Scotland, notably in the light of a case featuring several Deaf defendants and witnesses which was eventually dropped after the authorities deemed it necessary that seven interpreters be found to handle the case effectively. Seven interpreters at one case was a tall order which the service-providing bodies simply could not achieve.

But is this kind of approach altogether helpful? There are some outcomes that could be less than ideal. These relate in particular to the creation of co-constructed exchanges. Imagine the scene: two Deaf defendants are in the dock watching a third Deaf person giving witness testimony. Each defendant has been assigned his/her own interpreter to watch. The witness is watching a third interpreter. A question is directed to the witness: he/she sees this question as rendered by one interpreter. Each defendant sees the same question as rendered by a different interpreter. When the witness replies, the defendants look directly at the witness to see his/her answer.

There is clearly room for slippage here. The question that the defendants see answered is not the one that they saw posed. Since interpretation is necessarily a matter of interpretation, and we know how much every single nuance of language matters in a court of law, from the Deaf defendants' perspective there is a very real possibility of misconnections between questions and answers. (To compound this, the answer that the lawyer hears and uses in framing his/her next question is not the one any of the Deaf people saw given.) With this in mind, the successful outcome of the 'one Deaf person—one interpreter' policy cannot be assured.

Interpreter editing

Although the court operates on the basis of the 'convenient fiction' that the interpreter produces language that reflects all and only what was uttered in the source language, it would be an inhuman interpreter who could actually achieve this. Indeed, it is part of the very nature of interpreting as a process that there must be room for the interpreter to seek out that expression which seems, to him/her, to be most communicatively efficient in any given context.

However, this is not to deny that interpreters ever edit the source-language message in ways that can lead to confusion, inadequacy or miscommunication. To give just a single, simple example from the many that are collected in our primary data, it seems to us that the interpreter—acting for the court in one of the cases we observed—who heard the judge's phrase 'there is a clear and safe inference that…" and, as an interpretative equivalent, produced "means that", cannot be said to have maintained in the target language all of the salient elements of the source language message. Of course, the phrase was not 'an easy one' to deal with. Of course, other people present had their opportunity to object or otherwise comment. Of course, the interpreter may have been tired or simply made a human mistake. Despite all of these caveats, the fact is that in this context, the implications of 'clear and safe inference' are not trivial and their meaning should without question have been as clear in the signed interpretation as it was in the English-language original utterance.

What happens if the interpreter 'becomes present'?

With the best of will and skill in the world, there are always going to be times when the interpreter needs to set aside the strict neutral role in which he/she makes no self-generated contribution to the proceedings. This is particularly true when the interpreter needs, for any reason, to seek clarification of a signed or spoken utterance from one of the primary parties.

The problem for the interpreter in any such situation is how to make certain that it is clear to the audience—watching or listening—who it is that is in fact responsible for the content of the original source message. Thus, if a question is posed—hypothetically, "How many people were present at the fire?'—and the interpreter relays the question in BSL, watches the signed response, and then says "I'm sorry, do you mean when it started or later?" how is the court to know whether this is an utterance generated by the interpreter or generated by the Deaf witness and conveyed to the court by the interpreter?

Once again, this is an issue which can result in participants having a distorted view of the sequencing and coherence of the proceedings, and can thus be extremely confusing and disorientating. This is most sharply true when reference is made to the interpreter himself/herself by others in the court. Suddenly the interpreter's carefully constructed 'neutral' persona—i.e. "when I point at myself I am really referring to the speaker: when I say 'I' or 'me' I am really referring to the signer: the interpreter has no 'self' in this context"—comes apart at the seams. Without extraordinary care being taken to maintain the clarity of referents and points of reference, the interpreter can easily be drawn into a structural linguistic hall of mirrors where "I" does not mean "this I" but another "I" except when it does mean "this I"… and so on.

Interpreter using simcom as if to check voice-over

In our observations we sometimes noticed interpreters using the fact that their two languages occupy different modalities as if to check the accuracy of their interpretations with the Deaf viewer(s). That is, the interpreter would watch a Deaf witness' answer to a spoken question and would produce on their hands, face, et cetera, a version of that BSL answer in English for the consideration of the court whilst producing a simultaneous incomplete signed rendition of the answer being spoken.

Is this a satisfactory procedure? First of all, is the court aware of what is going on? Does it approve? We have never seen nor been given evidence of any court being appraised of the use of simultaneous communication (simcom) in this way. Is this something other non-English speakers are allowed? Second, is this actually a process that is likely to produce good results even where employed? Crucially, is the simcom rendition likely to be linguistically rich enough to convey all that is intended? As we saw above, if it is not, it is quite likely that the Deaf person would not indicate as much before the court (for reasons to do with the size and nature of the Deaf community, social and historical pressures, power issues, and so forth). Yet the very fact that the interpreter has, from his/her own point of view, given the Deaf person a chance to correct any mistakes—and no correction has been made—seems, on the face of it, to give reassurance that all is well. This may or may not be the case. There is abundant evidence that simcom is not the most efficient communicative vehicle in interaction between Deaf and hearing persons.

Initial recommendations

It doesn't take all that much attention before one realises that there is the potential in the circumstances we have catalogued above—and we believe this is only scratching the surface of the problems—for justice to be miscarried. To take just one illustrative example, think of a Deaf witness we watched in the court. He/she admitted to having lied in parts of his/her evidence. He/she was, in part, supposedly interviewed by the police in written English and in court made clear that he/she couldn't understand these texts. He/she was interviewed by the police on at least two occasions using at least two different interpreters. He/she was cross-examined in the lower courts using another two interpreters. He/she was cross-examined in a higher court using two interpreters who had already been exposed to his/her evidence at earlier stages of the case. This witness was asked which of the accounts he/she had given was accurate. We know that he/she may have lied, been confused or been misinterpreted at any stage. The opportunities for slippage, obfuscation and miscommunication are just staggering. No record was kept on videotape of any of this interaction. Is this safe justice?

1 There is insufficient information for Deaf people entering the legal system—whether as witnesses, complainants or suspects—concerning their rights and duties. Such information should be made available wherever possible in the signed languages which are most accessible to Deaf people.
2 We recommend that both Deaf Associations and Interpreters' Associations should make the strongest possible representations in an effort to secure within the legal system the services of interpreters who are (a) trained in the fundamentals of the interpreting task, (b) educated as legal specialists, (c) properly professional and (d) suitably monitored when undertaking such stressful and intense work.
3 We suggest that more care and attention should be paid to ensuring that interpreters are aware of the proper limitations of their role in the court setting, particularly in the matter of 'educating' the court about sign language issues. An interpreter, hired as an interpreter, shows little regard for the consequences of his/her action if he/she allows himself/herself to become drawn into the role of general advisor or consultant to the legal representatives on all matters pertaining to Deaf people.
4 It is clear that juries cannot be expected to know in any great depth

about the nature of signed language, Deaf culture and the Deaf community. Yet more time could certainly be taken—cf the trial involving the tycoon Robert Maxwell's sons, where the jury were instructed at length in the finer points of accountancy and financial management—to ensure that jurors do have relevant information at an early stage in any trial so that they may reach fair verdicts in cases involving Deaf people.

5 It is also our view at this stage that there is a need for education in issues relating to the nature of signed language and Deaf culture and the conduct of bilingual, bimodal interaction for legal professionals (police, solicitors, officers of the court, barr!isters, probation officers, judges et cetera).

6 Deaf people in the legal system are disadvantaged to the extent that no record is kept of their signed statements (only of the interpretation of these statements). We consider it to be imperative in the interests of securing just and safe verdicts that video-recordings should be made of all stages of legal interaction (including interviews with police officers and solicitors as well as courtroom exchanges).

7 Deaf people in the legal system are disadvantaged to the extent that much of the material upon which their case will have to be built is inaccessible to them since it is available only as written texts. It is vital that the courts recognise the right to have relevant transcripts translated onto videotape.

We have discussed issues relating to access to justice for Deaf people with a large number of persons working in the field. One view among legal professions seems to be that those who advocate on behalf of the Deaf community are 'making a political issue out of it'. One view on the Deaf side is that the judicial system is tring to pretend that these are merely legal matters with no political edge.

Our research suggests that there is something to be said on both sides. The legal issues cannot be properly and safely resolved without paying attention to the politics of language. The political agenda will not meet with the success it seeks unless it clearly demonstrates that it aims fundamentally to uphold the law and promote justice. Where issues of legality and politics meet—as they surely do in the cases we have covered in our research—then we suggest that the clear implication must be that what we face here is a human rights issue.

Project funding

This research was part of the *Access to Justice for Deaf People in the Bilingual, Bimodal Courtroom* project funded by The Leverhulme Trust.

Acknowledgments

This research would not have been possible without the goodwill of the interpreters and Deaf people observed and interviewed in the course of the research and the willingness to assist of personnel in the courts which we attended. The project also acknowledges the support of ASLI, SASLI, CACDP, BDA and RAD and the generous co-operation of Glasgow and West of Scotland Society for the Deaf, Strathclyde Regional Council, RNID (Scotland) and St. Vincent's Society for the Deaf in Glasgow.

Index

A

ADSUP. *See* Alliance of Deaf Service Users and Providers
advocacy 118
agencies 26, 29, 30, 43–48, 51, 65, 67, 119, 120
Alker, D. 22
Alliance of Deaf Service Users and Providers 115, 117
ally 12, 82
altruism 8
ambiguity 138, 191
analytical 12, 17, 19, 129
Anderson, P. 26
Anthony, D. 128
ASLI. *See* Association of Sign Language Interpreters
assessment 67, 90
Association of Sign Language Interpreters 28, 35, 98, 146, 182
assumption 12, 28, 64, 103, 137, 171
attitude 67, 103, 134, 162
audience 69, 70, 71, 81, 146, 204, 208, 212
authority 39, 49, 106, 112

B

BABELEA 18
Bailey, H. 66
Baker-Shenk, C. 154, 160
Barnes, L. 75
barrister 134, 171–177, 180, 186, 189, 191, 192, 195, 198, 199, 204–208
Bennett, A. 168
Bergman, B. 128
Berk-Seligson, S. 126, 129–132, 134, 136, 139, 143, 144, 145, 161, 163, 165
Bertling, T. 26
Bickerton. *See* Taylor, C.
bimodal 124, 134, 139, 142–146, 152, 154, 161, 162, 165, 169, 199, 210, 215

Blair, T. 22, 24, 25
Bornstein, H. 128
Bowis, J. 106, 115
Brace, A. 41
Bramwell, R. 104
Brennan, M. 8, 33, 41, 66, 76, 98, 125, 137, 145, 146, 165
Brien, D. 8, 66, 145, 146, 165
Brown, R. 8, 33, 41, 66, 76, 145, 146
business 12, 23, 35, 38, 47, 136, 144, 162, 179
Butler, I. 129, 153

C

Caccamise, F. 131
CACDP. *See* Council for the Advancement of Communication with Deaf People
Cameron, D. 124
Campaign for Real Interpreting 13
Canadian Freedom of Choice Movement 126
Chapman, G. 7
children 84, 89–98, 105–108, 113–115, 168, 172
Chu, E. 145, 165
client 17, 18, 37, 38, 41, 45, 49, 68, 104, 107, 112, 116–120, 159, 182
co-construction 138–140, 157, 160
Code of Ethics 8, 54, 67, 93, 107, 117, 160, 164
Code of Practice 39, 57, 98, 114–117, 155
coherence 191, 212
Cokely, D. 75, 79, 93
Collins, J. 66
Communication Support Worker 89
community interpreting 18
competence 15, 67, 80, 84, 91–95, 125, 134, 143, 144, 153
conduit 10, 11, 155–158, 160–163
conference interpreting 17, 18, 68
conspiracy of silence 55, 65
consumers 22, 24, 34, 35, 53, 65, 70, 71, 159, 160

conversation 76, 140, 155, 158, 160, 186, 197
Cooke, M. 55
Cornes, A. 66
Corsellis, A. 125
Council for the Advancement of Communication with Deaf People 26–30, 35, 39, 40, 44–47, 54, 67–78, 82, 83, 91–96, 98, 107, 113, 116–118, 126, 146, 155, 164
Court 30, 62, 63, 125–131, 143, 146, 153, 176, 183, 197, 199, 204
Coutts, K. 115
Crompton, R. 37, 38, 39
Crystal, D. 131
cultural mediation 60, 61, 189
culture 38, 40, 64, 67, 168, 169, 178, 182, 183, 207, 215
curriculum 15, 74, 80, 85, 87
Curtis, P. 103

D

Darby, A. 115
Davey, K. 26
Davies, A. 50
DDA. *See* Disability Discrimination Act
Deaf community 22, 23, 25, 30, 37, 46–49, 59, 112–115, 120, 130, 135, 152, 168, 182, 188, 195, 213, 215
Deaf consumers 35
Deaf culture 168, 169, 182, 215
Deaf perspective 169, 172–178, 183, 187, 188, 194, 200–205
Deaf Welfare Examination Board 113
decision-making 12, 63
demand 25, 58, 96, 143
Demjanjuk trial 127
Denmark, C. 8
dialogue 8, 59, 139, 140, 158, 160, 191
dilemmas 15, 35, 53–56, 63–65, 118
disability 103, 112, 116
Disability Discrimination Act 49, 50, 103–120
Disability Living Allowance 30, 49–51
discourse 79, 132–140, 152, 157, 191–195
DLA. *See* Disability Living Allowance
doctor 57, 58, 114, 159
DWEB. *See* Deaf Welfare Examination Board
Dykes, F. 103

dynamic 12, 55, 133

E

Eades, D. 132, 134, 135, 136, 145, 165, 194
Edexcel 86
Ellwood, J. 75
employment 35, 45, 51, 84, 89, 91, 92, 107, 129
equal opportunity 45, 105
equivalence 137
error 59, 68, 70, 78, 138, 144, 196, 199, 201, 205
ethics 18, 64, 70, 93, 107, 117
Etzioni, A. 26
evaluation 154
examination 82, 154, 196
expectation 17, 31, 60, 78, 80, 85, 103–106, 120
eyegaze 134, 136, 186

F

face 31, 63, 65, 79, 142, 153, 170, 213, 216
fee 43, 44, 45, 46, 47, 84
female 47, 65
Fenton, S. 37
footing 67, 86
foreign 197
Forsman, H. 66
Fowler, D. 94
freelance 43–51, 67, 109
Frishberg, N. 79, 154, 156, 158, 160, 165
Fryer, N. 103

G

gender 109
Gibbons, J. 141
Giddens, A. 25
Giles, H. 134
Gilroy, P. 25
Goodwin, C. 139, 157
government 25, 28, 35, 50, 51, 84, 85, 89, 141
Graffam Walker, A. 141
Green, C. 84, 85, 89–91, 99
Green, J. 66
grey zone 9, 11, 65
Gustason, G. 128

index

H

HAC. *See* Human Aids to Communication
Halliday, R. 30, 49
Harman, A. 66
Hayes, P. 98
health 12, 46, 49, 50, 105, 106–109, 111, 115, 119
Heaton, M. 94
Heidelberger, B. 146
helper 155, 159–162
hesitation 186
history 6, 7, 16, 155, 183
Hoyle, E. 37
Hull, S. 66
Human Aids to Communication 77, 106, 117
human right 163, 197, 216
Humphries, T. 127

I

impartial 60, 114, 117, 127, 155, 165
implication 47, 49, 57, 61, 99, 105, 106, 108, 114, 115, 127, 139, 141, 146, 157, 188, 194, 207, 212, 216
inference 193, 212
integration 17, 19
intent 58, 79, 80, 81, 92, 179, 193
interaction 8, 10, 28, 57, 82, 94, 124, 129–146, 152–163, 168–173, 183, 191, 195, 202, 205–209, 213–215
interference 159, 177
intermediary 157
interpersonal 32
Islam, M. 126

J

Jaworski, A. 135
Johnson, K. 80, 93
Judge 128, 205
jury 170, 174, 176, 184, 185, 215

K

Kamasinski case 125, 197
Katschinka, L. 37
Kegl, J. 41
King, M.L. 27
Kluwin, T. 79, 98

L

lag 81, 135, 205
Lane, H. 25, 127
Lashmar, P. 35
Laster 141, 142, 143, 144, 163
Laster, K. 127
lecturer 74, 77, 79, 81, 87
Leeth, J. 130
legal 12, 15, 49, 84, 104, 114, 125, 127, 129, 134, 136, 141, 142, 144, 147, 153, 154, 161–168, 173–187, 193–210, 214, 215
legislation 26, 49, 106, 108, 143, 144, 153, 197
Levi, J. 141
lexis 145, 201
liaison interpreting 68
Lightbown, P. 124
linguistic 61, 78, 80, 85, 93–96, 104, 124–146, 152–157, 164, 191, 194, 210, 213
Lochrie, J. 128
Loftus, E. 133

M

machine 54, 55, 69
mainstream 17, 96
male 65
Manasse, H. 39
Manpower Services Commission 89, 91.
McDonough, P. 66
McIntire, M. 8, 15, 41, 130, 156, 159, 162, 165
McWhinney, J. 22, 23, 24, 25, 26
meaning 37, 38, 58, 129, 137, 139, 154, 157, 164, 169, 187, 189, 193, 194, 199, 201, 207, 212
mediation 12, 28, 32, 39, 60, 61, 65, 82, 97, 124, 130, 132, 138, 152, 156, 158, 160, 170, 175, 177, 187, 189, 210
medical 84, 106, 127
Mental Health 111
Merton, R. 38
metaphor 10, 158, 191
midwifery 103, 108
minority 23, 104, 109, 126, 130, 131, 146, 184
miscommunication 211, 214

model 10, 11, 54–59, 63, 85, 95, 97, 103, 127–130, 138, 154–163, 190, 191, 196
monitoring 36, 143, 144
Moody, B. 66
Morris, R. 127, 142, 144, 161, 162

N

NATED 90, 91
National Disability Council 50
National Health Service 105, 108, 111, 119
neutrality 130, 163
NHS. *See* National Health Service
Nicholson, S. 66
Nickerson, W. 84, 85, 89, 90, 91, 94, 99
Noaks, L. 129, 153
norm 109
Nusser, P. 129

O

O'Barr, W. 131, 132
off-beam 207
omission 81
overlapping talk 135, 209

P

Padden, C. 127, 146
Palmer, C. 41, 165, 193
Palmer, J. 133
Panel of Four 46, 77, 115, 117
paradigm 17
Parker, D. 126
participant 10, 32, 76, 78, 127, 128, 131, 134, 135, 139, 142, 155–162, 212
passive 155, 203
Patrie, C. 41
pay 44, 45, 46, 47, 50, 51, 94
performance 79, 145, 152, 158, 162
Perry, B. 96
Philip, J.M. 66
philosophy 47, 99
Pickard, N. 115
Pickersgill, M. 91, 96
Pöchhacker, F. 17
Polack, K. 125
Police 113, 153, 169, 184, 199, 207
policy 27, 40, 44, 45, 49, 51, 83, 98, 104, 105, 111, 113, 120, 152, 154, 159, 169, 211
politeness 136, 194
Pollitt, K. 27, 33, 34, 41, 66, 145, 165
position 10, 17, 22, 25, 26, 55, 56, 105, 125, 130, 160, 162, 172, 177, 209, 210
power 24, 30, 37, 55, 111, 129, 159, 213
pragmatic 25, 26, 58, 71
preparation 33, 81, 87, 142, 197
process 10, 13, 67, 68, 78, 81, 82, 99, 107, 126, 128, 137–145, 152–157, 171, 176, 179, 195, 199, 204, 210–213
processing 17, 134, 204
profession 7–16, 32–48, 53, 84, 94, 97, 115, 118, 141, 143, 154, 155, 163

Q

quality 9, 10, 22, 24, 28, 34–39, 44–47, 51, 71, 105, 107, 109, 113, 120, 134, 144, 152, 180, 181
quality assurance 36

R

RAD. *See* Royal Association in Aid of Deaf People
Reagan, R. 27
Real Interpreting 13
Reed, M. 33, 37, 41, 66, 145, 165
Register (of interpreters) 83, 113, 118
register (linguistic ~) 39, 61, 195, 196
Registered Qualified Sign Language Interpreter 82
Registered Trainee Sign Language Interpreter 68
registration 44, 53, 82, 83, 98
regulation 22, 36, 38, 39, 40, 41, 54, 98, 114
rehabilitation 112
relationship 8, 17, 22, 27, 31, 34, 35, 53
relevance 186
research 6, 9, 11, 18, 19, 66, 94, 103, 124, 141, 145, 146, 153, 156, 158, 168, 172, 174, 194, 196, 209, 215, 216
Resnick, S. 41
responsibility 11, 13, 22, 26–41, 46, 49–66, 92–97, 106, 111–120, 130, 141, 160, 162, 187

Reynolds, G. 66
Rieber, R. 141
rights 22, 25–34, 49, 103, 114, 117, 144, 163, 173–175, 197, 210, 214, 216
RNID. *See* Royal National Institute for Deaf People
Roberts, R. 41
role 11, 12, 18, 29, 35, 39, 53–62, 69, 78, 84, 87, 89–98, 104, 105, 115, 125, 127–131, 134, 138, 152–164, 179, 182, 203, 212, 214
Roy, C. 54, 79, 93, 130, 135, 139, 145, 154, 156, 157, 162, 163, 165
Royal Association in Aid of Deaf People 146
Royal National Institute for Deaf People 22, 23, 24, 34, 50, 76
RQSLI. *See* Registered Qualified Sign Language Interpreter
RTSLI. *See* Registered Trainee Sign Language Interpreter

S

Sanderson, G. 80, 95, 130, 156, 159, 162, 165
SASLI. *See* Scottish Association of Sign Language Interpreters
scenario 30, 31, 48, 54, 57, 58, 59, 60, 62, 63, 69, 108, 124, 138
Schegloff, E. 135, 139, 157
schema 72
Scott Gibson, L. 34, 37, 53, 60, 115, 126, 154, 165
Scottish Association of Sign Language Interpreters 28, 35, 39, 40, 146
self 27, 32, 36, 43, 44, 67, 70, 116, 140, 142, 157, 158, 162, 165, 181, 212
sense 10, 26, 28, 30, 31, 32, 41, 46, 53, 55, 71, 79, 81, 119, 139, 140, 142, 156, 159–161, 171, 172, 179, 180, 183, 184, 191, 196, 198, 201, 205
sensitive 22, 34
Shackle, M. 103
Silas, D. 145, 165
simcom 213
Simpson, S. 27, 113
Smith, A. 98
Social Work 117
social work 56, 84, 91, 115–119
sociolinguistic 157

sociology 38
source language 78, 93, 211, 212
spoken language 7, 8, 37, 82, 142, 158, 180, 186
standards 8, 18, 37, 38, 83, 92, 113, 114, 120, 143, 156
Stewart, D. 98
Stewart, L. 26
Stewart, W. 141
strategy 25, 58, 60, 127, 136, 138, 140, 194
stress 23, 25, 65, 71, 95
structure 93, 159, 191
student 8–12, 16, 66, 74–99
style 156, 187, 195, 196
support worker. *See* Communication Support Worker
Sutton-Spence, R. 137

T

target language 78, 79, 93, 212
Tate, G. 41, 59, 66
Taylor, C. 41
television 70, 84
terminology 23, 69, 173, 193
text 6, 12, 33, 70, 75, 77, 79, 116, 128, 132, 176, 187, 197, 198, 200, 201, 214, 215
Than, R. 66
Thatcher, M. 23, 25, 27, 35
theatre 28, 84, 195
theory 6, 11, 124, 209
third party 32
Thomas, C. 103
Thomson, A. 29
Thoutenhoofd, E.D. 146
Tiersma, P. 141
trainee interpreter 8, 11, 39, 47, 65, 83, 84, 94, 118, 126. *See also* Registered Trainee Sign Language Interpreter
training 8–15, 29, 37, 44–46, 54, 56, 82–99, 106, 114, 117, 124, 130, 142–144, 152–154, 169, 170, 179, 181, 184, 193
translation 69, 77, 79–82, 93, 103, 198, 199
transliteration 77, 79
triad 18
turntaking 142

U

UCLAN. *See* University of Central Lancashire
University of Central Lancashire 83, 94
University of Durham 66, 147
untrained interpreter
    107, 113, 114, 115. *See also* trainee interpreter
utterance 8, 78, 82, 132, 135, 136, 139, 157, 161, 173, 192, 201, 205–207, 212

V

visual 82, 128, 137, 138, 184–186, 189–196
vocabulary 70, 93, 131, 154, 171, 189

W

Wadensjö 139, 145, 156, 158, 160
wages 48
Webster 75
Winston 75, 81, 93, 95, 96, 97
Witter-Merithew 130, 154, 160
Woll 137
Woodward 146
working conditions 45, 46, 143

Z

Zanni 133